Indian Business Case Studies

Indian Business Case Studies

Volume II

V P PAWAR
BHAGYASHREE KUNTE
SRINIVAS TUMULURI

Indian Case Studies in Business Management

OXFORD
UNIVERSITY PRESS

Great Clarendon Street, Oxford, ox2 6dp,
United Kingdom

Oxford University Press is a department of the University of Oxford.
It furthers the University's objective of excellence in research, scholarship,
and education by publishing worldwide. Oxford is a registered trade mark of
Oxford University Press in the UK and in certain other countries

© ASM Group of Institutes, Pune, India 2022

The moral rights of the authors have been asserted

First Edition published in 2022

Published in the United States of America by Oxford University Press
198 Madison Avenue, New York, NY 10016, United States of America

British Library Cataloguing in Publication Data

Data available

Library of Congress Control Number: 2022938091

ISBN 978-0-19-286938-8

DOI: 10.1093/oso/9780192869388.001.0001

Dr R.R. Pachpande
[1947–2009]

'Education is the Soul of our society'

The series editors and the volume authors of the case volumes titled as 'Indian Business Case Studies' published by Oxford University Press have a deep sense of gratefulness while dedicating these case volumes to the memory of Dr Raghunath R. Pachpande, the founder of ASM Group of Institutes Pune, India.

It was with the untiring efforts and strategic vision of Dr R.R. (as he was known to his close friends and colleagues) which has been instrumental in ASM group adopting case methodology as a unique element in its pedagogy which motivated the faculty and students of ASM group of institutes to develop business case studies on Indian Businesses and use them to teach management subjects in all branches of Business Management studies.

Dr R.R. Pachpande was a leader beyond parlance and ahead of time in establishing educational institutes more so in higher studies in business management specifically in the industrial belts in the state of Maharashtra with a view to providing best of experiential learning to its students through closer interactions with business Units around.

Today ASM Group continues the great legacy of Dr R.R. Pachpande under the leadership of his successors and who have succeeded in taking ASM Group to global recognition as a unique group of institutes offering world-class education in all branches of Business Management.

This case volume is dedicated to the memories of late Dr R.R. Pachpande.

Contents

SECTION II: CASE STUDIES IN
FINANCE MANAGEMENT

SECTION III: CASE STUDIES IN MULTIDISCIPLINARY AREAS IN MARKETING, STRATEGY, AND OPERATIONS

Preface

Many universities and management institutes across the globe have adopted the case study methodology for teaching almost all branches of management studies since several decades. This trend has been seen in India also, wherein the Indian Institutes of Management (IIMs) and progressive management institutes in private sector have implemented case methodology as an important pedagogical tool in business management education.

However, there is a severe shortage in Indian business case studies faced by the B-schools in India and those global institutes associated with Indian academia. Majority of the case studies studied at IIMs and other A-grade B-schools in India are from situations in industries in foreign countries and have very little or no relevance to Indian business situations. This acts as a major gap for faculty and students engagement in business management studies both at UG and masters level (PG) studies, where in for clarification of theoretical concepts is possible mainly through use of case methodology which enables insight into business real-life business situations.

Besides, the objectives and purposes for which case studies are developed abroad are much different from course of studies in Indian B-schools. Therefore, the dependence on foreign case studies for Indian students does not provide any real situational insight on Indian business. Although the curriculum requires taking the students through case study methodology, there are not many Indian case studies for this purpose.

The main objectives of using case-based teaching as a major pedagogical tool in B-schools are as follows:

1. To facilitate students' concept development capabilities through exposure to real-life problems in industries.
2. To enable students to correlate theoretical topics with the techniques used in analysing complex issues in business situations.

3. To develop skills using which students can develop application matrix for the theoretical topics for real-life problem analysis and resolution techniques.
4. Help the students of B-schools to develop orientation towards the important attributes and attitudinal requirements for effective handling of complex situations at the workplace.
5. To develop a clear understanding of the techniques used for problem analysis, situation analysis, and decision analysis and appropriate understanding of the difference between problems and situations in management.
6. To develop the group-based approaches to solving problems and challenges at the workplace by appropriate coordination of and collaboration with all related aspects of a situation.
7. To develop a reference manual for recording the problems tackled and the essential lessons learnt from past incidences for use in future eventualities of recurrence of issues.
8. To develop the preventive steps that must be initiated to ensure the problems resolved once do not recur in the immediate future.

Business case studies are basically oriented towards developing the evaluative and analytical skills of students towards industry situations. Such case studies draw the attention of participants of the case resolution methodology on the in-depth correlative evaluation of the issues in the case study with the various related topics that the students have to study about in their classrooms. These case studies could be on issues related to human resources, industrial relations, product and process, marketing and finance management areas in business management.

The academic environment across the world too is facing a major disruption on account of the global pandemic Covid-19 forcing the offline education system to switch over to online/blended versions of teaching and learning process. And use of case methodology and simulation exercises are the main in gradients for sustaining effective ways of delivering experiential learning through use of case and case lets in an online mode of teaching ensuring student engagements and online interactive ways of knowledge dissemination.

Oxford University Press in association with ASM Group of Institutes Pune, India is publishing for the first time a comprehensive case volumes as series of eight volumes with case studies on Indian businesses selected from all aspects of business functions like HR, finance marketing, and operations providing an exciting and long waited opportunity to faculty and students across the globe to access Indian business case studies through these case volumes.

We are very confident that the case volumes will receive very good response and will be of utmost use to the readers.

Acknowledgements

The series editors wish to acknowledge with thanks the contribution of data for the case studies from ASM's Academic Associates the CETYS University Mexico—Dr Francisco Velez, Dean of Colleges and Dr Faviola Villegas Prof in marketing for case studies on Apple and Coca Cola as also several senior faculty from ASM Group of Institutes for their help in proofreading and editing of the case studies.

We also acknowledge the numerous reporters and of daily newspapers in business and economics scenarios in India which have been rich and authentic secondary data sources for design and development of case studies for the case volumes.

About the Series Editors

Dr Sandeep Pachpande, Chairman,
ASM Group of Institutes, Pune, India

Prof J.A. Kulkarni, Professor,
ASM Group of Institutes, Pune, India

Both the series editors have decades of experience in business case design and development and also implementation of case methodology of teaching for the faculty and students of business schools in India and abroad.

The series editors have to their credit of authoring three major books on business case studies published by globally known publishers and in conducting workshops for case design and development.

The series editors have a very good network with leaders and stalwarts in business management studies across the globe and popular as keynote speakers in many national and international conferences. They have a very rich experience in organizing national and international conferences and case competitions.

Currently the series editors are busy completing a unique case analysis and resolution methodology programme which is under copyright considerations.

Dr Sandeep Pachpande

Prof J.A. Kulkarni

About the Volume Authors

Dr V.P. Pawar

Dr V.P. Pawar is Director at the ASM Group of Institutes Pune, India.

Dr Pawar holds a PhD in Computer Science and is a (ES) Cambridge University alumnus (UK). He holds Post Doctorate degree in Artificial Intelligence, as well as a Master's Degree in Computer Science, Computer Application, and an MBA. Dr V.P. Pawar has 19 years of experience in the Government Sector as Super Class One Ranking Officer.

Dr Pawar has been conferred 11 fellowships in the field of science and technology from the privileged institutions such as DST (Department of Science and Technology, Government of India), UGRF (UGC), University of Cambridge (UK), Microsoft, Oracle Corporation, F.J Trust, Sakal Indian Foundation.

Dr Pawar has published more than 100+ international journals and conference proceedings in IEEE, Science Direct, Elsevier, and many more.

Dr Pawar is the recipient of 43 National and International Level Patents (Australia/USA/JAPAN and India). Dr Pawar guided 22 Doctoral students for PhD degrees.

Dr Pawar has keen interest in teaching and research case studies for management studies and he has been a senior jury in several case competitions.

Prof T Srinivas B.com, M.com

Prof T. Srinivas brings along with him nearly 25 years of industry experience in financial management at functional and strategic finance at board level responsibilities.

Since previous 15 years Prof Srinivas has been an integral member of the senior faculty at ASM Group of Institutes Pune engaged in course and subject syllabus for graduate and postgraduate level studies in finance and taxation management.

Prof Srinivas has presented several research papers in national and international conferences and has designed and developed several business case studies on topics such as investment banking, assets management, and taxation issues. He also has authored few case studies in strategic management and corporate governance.

Prof Srinivas is an authority in all topics related to finance and financial accounting and his help and guidance is sought after by several of his colleagues and students from Finance Management Stream.

Dr Bhagyashree S. Kunte MBA Finance, FCMA, PhD
(Faculty: Commerce and Financial Management)

Dr Bhagyashree Kunte brings with her nearly 15 years of industry experience at management level in the functions of finance management she has rich exposure to managerial finance and in overall project financing responsibilities in several Indian companies of repute.

Over the previous 10 years Dr Bhagyashree has rendered her services in Finance Management subjects for the UG and PG level studies. She has to her credit several research papers presented in national and international level conferences along with her keen interest in adopting case methodology of teaching to her students in financial accounting and decision science subjects. She has designed and developed case studies in banking and taxation management topics.

The How and Why of Case Methodology

An insight in to the use of case methodology in B school pedagogy.

Case Methodology in Business Management Studies

The main objectives of using case-based teaching as a major pedagogical tool in B-schools are as follows:

1. To facilitate students' concept development capabilities through exposure to real-life problems in industries.
2. To enable students to correlate theoretical topics with the techniques used in analysing complex issues in business situations.
3. To develop skills using which students can develop application matrix for the theoretical topics for real-life problem analysis and resolution techniques.
4. To help the students of B-schools to develop orientation towards the important attributes and attitudinal requirements for effective handling of complex situations at the workplace.
5. To develop a clear understanding of the techniques used for problem analysis, situation.
6. To analysis and decision analysis and appropriate understanding of the difference between problems and situations in management.
7. To develop the group-based approaches to solving problems and challenges at the workplace by appropriate coordination of and collaboration with all related aspects of a situation.

8. To develop a reference manual for recording the problems tackled and the essential lessons learnt from past incidences for use in future eventualities of recurrence of issues.
9. To develop the preventive steps that must be initiated to ensure the problems resolved once do not recur in the immediate future.

Major Types of Case Studies

The entire gamut of business case studies can be classified as follows:

1. Evaluative case studies (Teaching Case studies)
2. Task- or action-oriented case studies (including project-based case studies)
3. Research-oriented case studies

Evaluative or teaching case studies are basically oriented towards developing the evaluative and analytical skills of students towards industry situations. Such case studies draw the attention of participants of the case resolution methodology on the in-depth correlative evaluation of the issues in the case study with the various related topics that the students have to study about in their classrooms.

These case studies could be on issues related to human resources, industrial relations, product and process, marketing and finance management areas in business management. Such case studies help the students mainly to examine their understanding of evaluative steps such as evaluation of the financial situation of a company or the quality aspects of its products and services, etc.

The task- or action-oriented case studies dwell on business issues that call for appropriate decision-making capabilities of executives. By involving students of management studies in the resolution activity of such case studies, the skills learnt by them through the theoretical studies can be experimented in the resolution exercises. The students can be motivated to apply their decision-making skills along with their risk management ability to make business decisions.

Developing a plan of actions oriented towards the resolution of the case issues calls for effective role-play techniques as also presentation skills from the part of students; they are normally required to defend their plan of approach and decisions in front of other students and the faculty, which helps them improve their capabilities to sustain questions and criticisms, normal features in business management.

Research-based case studies, as the name suggests, involve students in research initiatives to establish a hypothesis or to disprove a common belief, which influence the progress and sustenance of business ideologies or even scientific or technical aspects of business dynamics.

These case studies normally call for prerequisites such as thorough business knowledge and enough exposure to both the theoretical and practical aspects of the issues presented in the case studies. Issues of corporate governance and social welfare functions, which have both obligatory and voluntary elements attached to them, are pursued in research studies to establish the utility purposes of such aspects, which range from free will to a compelled activity.

Market-survey case studies help students to differentiate between facts and fantasies of customer behaviour and understand the competitive forces at play in the marketplace. Business environmental analysis and the study of business options and strategic choices are recommended areas for case studies calling for research.

However, the real problem today for B-schools is the non-availability of good case studies on Indian business. Since the usage of imported case studies from foreign businesses is fast losing its relevance to the Indian business scenario, which in itself has unique features among the global economies. India, which is rated as the world's fourth-largest economy, definitely needs specific and separate approaches to the case study methodology as a pedagogical tool for B-school studies.

This also calls for intensifying the industry-institute interactions at least at the B-school level of education. Both sides need to shed their shy or protective nature to facilitate effective and purposeful interactions.

Even the government, and specifically the department of higher education, needs to emphasize the absolute need for closer contacts between the higher educational institutes and the business houses in all segments of the economy. Only then can the studies at higher level be compatible to the needs of businesses and the educational degrees or qualifications be worthy of any application in the real economic progress of India, based on domestic skills as relevant to business needs.

Case studies in business management are characterized by their relevance to the theories and practices of businesses across the world. While there could be cultural differentiation, the need is to align with the basic purpose of business ventures. Men, machines, and materials form the basic resources of a business, and customers at the relevant marketplace create the necessary turnover of these resources.

Every business or entrepreneurial venture is preceded by the necessity of there being means for survival and creation of wealth by the stakeholders. It is in a way a mixture of needs, actions, and results in a perpetual series and cycle of events, which consume and recreate themselves for the continuity of life on this planet perhaps.

Case Study: Design and Development Methodology

Every business or entrepreneurial venture is preceded by the necessity of there being means for survival and creation of wealth by the stakeholders. It is in a way a mixture of needs, actions and results in a perpetual series and cycle of events, which consume and recreate themselves for the continuity of life on this planet perhaps.

The case studies in business management depend very much on the 'virtual' nature of their contents, and the actual and real-life demonstration of business situations that they bring to the classroom in business schools help in letting the students correlate the theoretical and practical aspects of business management.

Case studies should generate interest in the minds of students and awake in them a curiosity to understand the contents of a case study and an urge to involve oneself in the case analysis and resolution process. Then only can case studies be called effective tools that translate real-life business scenarios to classroom discussion topics.

The case studies in business management are characterized by features as follows:

1. Fact-based contents and narrations rather than fantasies and fiction.
2. Necessity of an appropriate 'hook effect' in case contents and the chronological presentation of a case.
3. Presence of just enough ambiguity and vagueness in the deliberations of the case.
4. Providing clues and not exact solutions to case issues.
5. Providing specificity in the comparison and correlation of case contents to topics of studies in business management.

Case study Based on Facts

In order to make a case study present a real-life situation, it should necessarily be based on the facts of a business situation, either a past situation or a concurrent happening in the domestic or international business environment. However, in order to protect an individual's or an organization's business interests, one may, to the maximum extent possible, camouflage the names of individuals, organizations or the exact product and process nomenclatures, besides duly respecting the copyrights of the owners of the references made, if any, in the case contents.

The students of business management definitely desire to feel involved when they have to study, analyse, and resolve business case studies; hence, any distortion in the facts, details not confirming to regular business transactions or issues not commonly visualized during the course of their studies tend to deflect their focus and create a sense of artificiality or disinterest in their approach to the case study methodology.

In fact, this is one of the most important reasons why case studies based on industrial situations abroad are of lesser interest to the students of Indian B-schools, since they do not depict real business scenarios in the Indian business environment and are deprived of the cultural relevance so essential to Indian students.

It is also observed that in many a case study, an attempt is made by the authors of the case study to dramatize the narration to such an extent that the seriousness of the topic in relation to business management studies is completely disregarded. And such case studies are remembered by the students for their fun content rather than facts of business life. This has an implied risk in that students may totally miss the objective of the case study methodology of business management studies and consider case studies as irrelevant to business studies' requirements.

A good case study, therefore, should necessarily draw the attention of students to the events and facts normally reported in the business magazines or based on reports appearing in the newspapers, a journals, such that the students' natural interests are aroused to know more about the issues involved through case analysis and discussions. Students who are aware of the happenings in the business world around them will be happy to clarify their understanding of the theoretical aspects of their course of management studies by making the best use of case study methodology.

Necessity of 'Hook Effect' in Business Case Studies

For a film to be entertaining and interesting till the last scene, it must capture the imagination of the audience and make them feel as though they are a part of the environment created by the film; similarly, it is necessary that business case studies create a feeling in the students that they are a part of the case study from the beginning to the final resolution. This is the essential hook effect that every case study in business management should strive to achieve.

Mind well that this does not mean the authors should resort to fantasizing the narration of case contents; the purpose of films is pure entertainment, whereas the purpose of business case studies is to develop a strong sense of attachment of the student towards case contents, as is relevant to their course of studies; it is in their own interests to understand the analysis and resolution process of a particular case study that looks so similar to real-life business situations about which they have some knowledge.

Case studies in business management should provide enough opportunities for conflicts and disagreements, lively discussions, and competitive team spirit among the students. The case studies should also generate an interest in the students to look out for additional data from sources such as the Internet and business magazines, balance sheets of companies, etc., to gather further information to help them understand management concepts and prepare them to provide effective analysis and resolutions to the questions raised by the case writer.

Every business executive necessarily suffers much anxiety and related stressful situations in the resolution of day-to-day problems at the workplace. The purpose of business case studies is to simulate an environment that is as real as possible using the case content and analysis and resolution process.

'Ambiguity and Vagueness' in Business Cases

A professional manager often comes across ambiguous and vague situations including discontinuous changes in their day-to-day activities. In fact, these situations incite creative and innovative responses from the managers, leading to ensuring sustainability amidst volatile market forces. If every step is based on logic and must be preplanned or doctored, then perhaps life will not be worth living it.

In the parlance of strategic management, we often talk of change management and of 'discontinuous changes', which defy logic and sense of sequencing of events. The real capability factors for effective business management are the ones that can manage business uncertainties like never before in globalized competitive environments. It is these uncertainties, which are the real ambiguities and vagueness in business management, that the case studies are supposed to imbibe while the students are on the lookout for logical steps in analysis and issue resolution.

Case studies should induce the students to think outside the box for the resolution of issues for a given situation. A case study should not be a drab story from cradle to grave or a reincarnation of business practices, which kills the creative capabilities of students and oversimplifies the challenges faced in effective business management. The case studies should deflect logic-based thinking to change management areas wherein the students are required to play different roles in providing long-term solutions to the issues mentioned in the case studies. Questions such as why, when, how, how much, who, etc., should naturally surface while analysing and resolving case issues.

'Clues' for Case Analysis and Resolution

Providing clues and soft hints along the sequence of events in case study analysis and resolution will enable students to direct their analyses towards the objectives of the case study. It is often the experience that students lose their focus on important aspects of the case study and start drifting towards issues on less critical points.

This is also quite often the case in real-life industry situations wherein the major focus in important discussions gets deflected to trivial issues, resulting in wastage of valuable time, conflicts of interests, and escalation of the problem rather than arriving at any resolution. Business case studies should make special attempts to keep the focus of the analysis and resolution methodology oriented on major issues.

This can be done by proper sequencing of events in the case study such that the readers of the case are provided with links to the theme of the case as frequently as required by providing clues to the root causes for the issues and hints to the likely solution or answers to the questions asked by the case writer.

For example, if the case writer wants the students to compare the case issues with 'competitive strategy' situations, then the mention of 'competitive environment' as an often repeated data or issue in the case study would keep the students focused in their analysis and discussions on, say, the 'competitive advantage matrix', as enumerated by Michel Porter on strategic business management topics.

Similarly, case studies in human resources (HR) should provide clues on HR-related issues, rather than constantly talking about competition and product-related issues. Of course, in the case of case studies in overall operations management including mergers and acquisitions, it would be prudent to provide related clues on each functional area and the respective topics in classroom studies.

Nevertheless, should the clues attempt to mislead the participants, the very belief and credibility of the case study methodology of studies would be destroyed. It is also equally important to note that the clues should only be indicative and not directive in their purpose.

Case Teaching Notes

Case study teaching notes are primarily for the case instructor or the faculty who use the case study methodology for teaching business management topics to students. Following are some of the important aspects of case teaching notes (these are not exclusive in their coverage; the concerned faculty could add, delete, or modify the same to make their case teaching process as effective as possible):

Every case presenter should provide students with a brief summary of the case in order to generate initial awareness and prepare the students to study the case as a cursory note or a preamble of their expectations from the analysis and resolution efforts required for the case study.

A list of the main topic and sub-topics intended to be taught through the particular case study needs to be prepared and discussed beforehand by the faculty with the students, in order to ensure there is enough clarity of understanding and expectations from a particular case study.

Reference to important theories such as Maslow's theory, Herz Berg's theory, Michel Porter's model on business competitive and market forces, GE 9 cell model for investment decisions, etc., in any other specialization area of business management studies should be made in a separate 'Focus of Studies' part of the teaching notes and should be shared with the students in advance of case study discussions to enable the students to consolidate their understanding and applicability of a particular theory during the analysis and resolution process of case study discussions.

The teaching notes should also contain corollary topics and references to other aspects of the course of studies, which may not have been covered in the main case content. Additional information about a product, process, or business unit or comparisons with similar real-life situations and relevant market situations, if available with the faculty, is shared with the concerned students; this will help the students to correlate their knowledge with this additional information, which refers to an actual situation.

Every faculty should necessarily collect feedback from the groups or individuals who have studied the case and their comments on the utility of the case study towards their course of business management studies must be noted. This feedback will help the faculty to make necessary improvements in leading the case study by answering certain observations made by the participants.

Every faculty should prepare an assignment case study to be completed by the students, to encourage students to experience the work life through exercises in case study resolutions.

Prevalent Methods for Case Analysis and Resolution

Case study methods used for providing clarity on management concepts mostly focus on either imaginary situations or events based on records of failures or successes in the organizational setup. Besides, the approach for case-studies resolution has often focused merely on 'SWOT' analysis (SWOT stands for strengths, weaknesses, opportunities, and threats involved in a project) of an organization with a lesser degree of focus on failures in areas such as strategic decision making, strategic planning, and compatibility in organizations to strategic approach and implementation. The issues in strategically managed companies basically emanate from weaknesses in strategic thinking and a systematic approach to problem resolution.

As Dr Peter Drucker, the management guru, says: 'Management of many business units are busy resolving yesterday's problems today. And there is hardly any clarity between problems and opportunity.' He continues: 'Business investments for competitive advantage need to focus on investments in opportunities rather than in problems.' It is observed that many business organizations take comfort in handing over to the consultants the real problems of the organization. In the first instance, there is no reason for problems to exist if one is to ensure strategic correction during the implementation of strategies in ongoing or new business ventures.

The consultants, in many cases, help expedite the early death of such businesses with their third-party approach (lack of involvement and commitment) to the issues referred and their practice of extracting hefty charges for their consultancy reports, most of which are vague prescriptions (glorified 'sounds good'—type recommendations) that help boardrooms feel happy that their future is secured.

However, in today's globalized competitive business environment, the top management needs to lay special emphasis on attending present issues, focusing on the resolution of present issues, burying past problems with appropriate strategy implementation, and preparing for the future, which calls for competitive advantage capabilities.

Further, many companies like business process outsourcing (BPO) companies, knowledge process outsourcing (KPO) companies, and multinational companies (MNCs) are under the clutches of the managerial autocratic ('do as we say') approach. This reduces the creativity of their employees, and converts them to mere 'robots' in their attitudes and presentations. Today, from middle school to management studies logic-based computer-aided business planning processes are being emphasized rather than creativity-enhancing involvements that call for human endeavour in attaining success and satisfaction.

Understanding the major working details of any organization entails the collection of relevant data from sources such as present status and past record of organizational health. In majority of cases, we need to analyse the past performance data. As in the case of biological issues, in an organizational life history there are events and episodes that occur as major factors inhibiting the progress or causing the decline of the organization; in such cases, often the management had no clue or controlling authority over the organization to understand the issues or prevent the decline in advance.

Diagnosing these maladies affecting an organization is comparable to a doctor conducting diagnostic investigation into the serious ailments of his or her patient. For serious ailments (excepting epidemics and contagious diseases), all factors and issues that influence the malady are personal habits, malnutrition, hygiene factors, and also immunity factors developed during the past period that are either protective or provocative to health or sickness, respectively.

Case History Details

1. Symptoms: Present and past, as recorded.
2. Historical data: Business past history, including all important factors such as details of promoters, financing, products, prices, and marketing.

3. Factors influencing performance:
   a. Congenital factors: Family background (erstwhile business promoters, vision, mission, and objectives); any effects of 'success sclerosis' (arrogance due to affluence from past success), or 'points of inflection' as is called in business terms, could be factors that go unrecognized in the present malady.
   b. Professionalization and management thoughts on fresh approach, skill-building, and competence factors: These lead to the restless urge to change over from complacence to competence (in a competitive market situation) or from intolerance to infectivity of people and processes (as compared to the 'we too ran' attitude of the organization in the past).
   c. As in the case of diversification or acquisition and mergers, the issues could result from correct or defective selection of businesses (products and processes) or partners, the necessity to change, consequent changes in management capability, improvement anxiety syndrome, etc.
   d. Hurdles in succession planning: The 'Generation Next' may have different value systems (sometimes non-compatible with those of its predecessors) and not have a balanced or matured approach as seen by business observers.
   e. Fresh approach to business philosophy, a new vision or mission in light of the changing global economy: Both vertical and horizontal integrations (forward and backward integrations) aid typical expectations of the customers of the emancipated market environment.
   f. Inability to tolerate the impact of coexistence of new and old cultures.

The following logical, sequential, and important steps help to understand, in a comprehensive manner, analysis, and resolutions for a case study of any type of business or industry at both corporate and functional levels:

1. Data collection and segmentation (case details)
2. Discuss issues/dilemmas/problems involved in the case

3. Diagnosis (case analysis): Correlating issues of the case with relevant styles of narration in terms of management terminology, in practical business life and conducting a SWOT analysis if required
4. Case Resolution (issue resolution—resolutions and recommendations)
    a. Short term (intermediate steps): Damage control steps
    b. Long term (back to life): Regaining normal health
    c. Preventive steps (impact of implementing the recommendations)
        (i) Consequent prevention-oriented recommendations
        (ii) Building strategic capabilities in subjects (organization) to develop the capability to succeed and develop adequate immunity in case the challenge or malady repeats or has side effects in an altogether new dimension
5. Record of lessons learnt
    (a) Appropriate record of cause-and-effect analysis of issues (b). Record of probability analysis

Serial Number	Case History (Major Details)	Disease (Investigative Observation) Issues (Major) of the Case	Diagnosis (Relevance to Management Terminology)	Treatment		Preventive Measures (Prepared for Consequences If Any)	Lesson Learnt (Case Record for Future Ref- erence)
				short term	long term		

Stages/Areas of Activity	Tools Recommended
Strategy formulation	Vision, mission, objective orientation driver/business drivers/critical success factors
Strategic analysis	Environmental appraisal methods:
	Direct–indirect
	Macro–micro
	External–Internal stake Holders
	Organizational appraisal methods:
	SWOT analysis
	Risk analysis
	Boston Consultancy Group matrix
	GE 9 cell model
	For investment decisions
Strategic options	Acceptability
	Feasibility
	Flexibility
Strategic choice	Best choice matrix
	Must/wish drill
Strategic decisions	Decision matrix
	Decision tree
	Short- and long-term impact analyses
Strategy implementation	Operational control method
	Strategic control method
Strategy evaluation	Gap analysis
	Root cause analysis
	Probability factor analysis of present and potential effects
	Corrective steps
	Review progress
	Reconfirm strategic alignment

The case studies included in this **Case Volume II** are selected diligently to provide a very variety of businesses and issues involved in each of the cases being much different than the other. The chapters cover almost all types and segments of industry and markets providing a very good opportunity for the readers to refer to the aspects explained in this brief note on case methodology and its utility in concept clarification and exposure to experiential learning for the students of B schools as also to younger business executives up the career ladder.

SECTION I
CASE STUDIES IN HUMAN RESOURCES

HR, Entrepreneurship, CSR, CG, and Sustainability

1. The Culture vs Strategy
2. Tata's Air India 'Take Over to Take Off'—A Cultural Conundrum
3. Beyond the Bootstrap
4. Starbucks—The 'Coffee House' Experts
5. Great Thought—Difficult for Business

1

The Culture vs Strategy

A Case Study on Bosch India Ltd. IR Issues in the MNC

Learning Objectives

The given case helps us to understand the role of actors of industrial relations (IR) towards effective HRM in the organization. It analyses the compliance of the actors under the existing labour laws as applicable to the organization. It comprehends the attitude of employees, employers, and industry towards each other and also towards the job. It focuses on the nuances of people management function and its contribution towards the violence that eventually resulted in lockout. To comprehend various organizational behaviour concepts that shall help synergize the employees' objectives and employer's goal to analyse the complete incident with relevant organizational and IR theories.

Synopsis

This case describes an Industrial Relations (IR) situation in an automobile company in India. It begins with the mention of incidents which begins with lockout at the company. A lockout is a temporary work stoppage or denial of employment initiated by the management of a company during a labour dispute. According to the rule, after the company's lockout, workers are not paid till the time it (lockout) is revoked. The monthly salaries of its employees for the period before the incident will be paid only after the lockout is withdrawn and the plant starts functioning. The case highlights the growing number of instances of clashes between the employees and the management of companies in India, due to unjustified

Indian Business Case Studies. V P Pawar, Bhagyashree Kunte, and Srinivas Tumuluri, Oxford University Press.
© ASM Group of Institutes, Pune, India 2022. DOI: 10.1093/oso/9780192869388.003.0001

demands by the workers which are often guided by external parties such as trade unions and political parties. German automobile component manufacturer Bosch has declared a lockout at its Jaipur plant due to an 'illegal go-slow' action since 19 March 2015 and on an indefinite hunger strike by the union office bearers.

About Bosch

The Bosch Group is a leading global supplier of technology and services. It employs roughly 375,000 associates worldwide (as of 31 December 2015). According to preliminary figures, the company generated sales of more than 70 billion euros in 2015. Its operations are divided into four business sectors: mobility solutions, industrial technology, consumer goods, and energy and building technology. The Bosch Group comprises Robert Bosch GmbH and its roughly 440 subsidiaries and regional companies in some 60 countries. If its sales and service partners are included, then Bosch is represented in roughly 150 countries. This worldwide development, manufacturing, and sales network are the foundation for further growth. In 2015, Bosch applied for some 5,400 patents worldwide. The Bosch Group's strategic objective is to deliver innovations for a connected life. Bosch improves the quality of life worldwide with products and services that are innovative and spark enthusiasm. In short, Bosch creates technology that is 'Invented for life'.

The company was set up in Stuttgart in 1886 by Robert Bosch (1861–1942) as 'Workshop for Precision Mechanics and Electrical Engineering'. The special ownership structure of Robert Bosch GmbH guarantees the entrepreneurial freedom of the Bosch Group, making it possible for the company to plan over the long term and to undertake significant up-front investments in the safeguarding of its future. Ninety-two per cent of the share capital of Robert Bosch GmbH is held by Robert Bosch Stiftung GmbH, a charitable foundation. The majority of voting rights are held by Robert Bosch Industrie Treuhand KG, an industrial trust. The entrepreneurial ownership functions are carried out by the trust. The remaining shares are held by the Bosch family and by Robert Bosch GmbH.

Bosch Company History

1. 1886–1900: The workshop for precision mechanics and electrical engineering
2. 1901–1923: Becoming a global automotive supplier
3. 1924–1945: From automotive supplier to diversified group
4. 1946–1959: Rebuilding and the economic miracle
5. 1960–1989: Founding of the divisions and breakthrough in electronics
6. 1990–2015: Solutions to the challenges of globalization

About Bosch in India

In India, Bosch is a leading supplier of technology and services in the areas of mobility solutions, industrial technology, consumer goods, and energy and building technology. Additionally, Bosch has in India the largest development centre outside Germany, for end-to-end engineering and technology solutions. The Bosch Group operates in India through nine companies, viz, Bosch Ltd., Bosch Chassis Systems India Ltd., Bosch Rexroth India Ltd., Robert Bosch Engineering and Business Solutions Pvt. Ltd., Bosch Automotive Electronics India Pvt. Ltd., Bosch Electrical Drives India Pvt. Ltd., BSH Home Appliances Pvt. Ltd., ETAS Automotive India Pvt. Ltd., and Robert Bosch Automotive Steering India Pvt. Ltd. In India, Bosch set up its manufacturing operation in 1953, which has grown over the years to include 14 manufacturing sites, and seven development and application centres. Bosch Group in India employs over 29,000 associates and generated consolidated revenue of about Rs 15,250 crores in 2014 of which Rs 10,800 crores from the third party. The Group in India has close to 12,000 research and development associates and has filed for around 150 patents in 2014. In India, Bosch Limited is the flagship company of the Bosch Group. It earned revenue of over Rs 9,570 crores in 2014.

Employees of Bosch Bangalore plant go on strike in March 2013.

The employee union of Bosch Ltd, MICO Employee's Association (MEA), has begun a 'tool down' strike at the Bosch Bangalore plant.

The company has called it illegal. The strike is the result of the suspension of a workman at the plant. The company, which makes automotive components and systems, has had a history of union unrest with the latest strike being the second such in the last 18 months.

A statement issued by Bosch read, 'It was observed that some associates deployed in a new production line were unwilling to meet basic production requirements in accordance with the standards of industrial engineering.'

'Over the past three months, the workmen adopted a "go-slow" approach producing significantly lower than earlier attained levels. After much deliberation, disciplinary action resulting in suspension of one of the identified workmen was taken.' The company added that it was in dialogue with the MEA and the labour commissioner to resolve the strike.

In October 2011, MEA had launched a similar 'tool down' strike to protest the company's decision to outsource certain non-core manufacturing and support processes from its Bangalore plant in a bid to reduce costs and competitively price its products.

In 2010 too there was a 'tool down' strike that led to Bosch declaring a complete lockdown after the union employees physically intimidated and threatened managers of the plant. The manufacturing sector, in particular the auto sector, has been witnessing major strikes around the country.

Bosch Bengaluru plant 'tool down' strike was called off in March 2013. The employee union of Bosch Ltd—MEA has called off the strike post discussion with the Bosch management on 9 March 2013. The management and the union meeting concluded with a quick resolution on the issues, supported by the intervention of Additional Labour Commissioner.

An agreement was reached on the working model for the new production line as per well-established industrial engineering standards. Based on this, the suspension of one employee has been withdrawn; however the enquiry on the employee will still continue. The workmen have resumed work at the factory premises starting from the night shift of 9 March 2013.

A quick resolution to the issues has been reached, however, practices like 'go-slow' and the illegal tool down strike, affecting the employees and the company must be avoided. Bosch Management stresses that in accordance with its reputation as a fair employer, all decisions pertaining to business shall be in favour of the organization and its employees. Bosch will continue to act fairly yet firmly in all such situations.

Bosch Strike: Talks with Management on 17 September 2014 to Resolve Issues

The first round of talks with the management would be held 18 September 2014 to resolve issues at German auto component major Bosch Ltd.'s Adugodi plant, where strike by workers entered the second day today, a union official said.

'We will be holding a bilateral talks with the management as per the direction of Additional Labour Commissioner Narasimhamurthy to solve issues pending for the past 22 months'—MEA president.

The workers had gone on tool down strike. After the bilateral meeting, a tripartite meeting, involving the union, the company management and the Additional Labour Commissioner, will be held on 20 September, he said.

The workers had gone on an indefinite strike claiming that the management planned to cut down some medical benefits and demanded productivity 'which cannot logically happen to the level of their expectation'. While the company in a filing to the BSE described the demands of the workers as 'unreasonable' and the strike is illegal. The company has 2,575 permanent workers, 700 temporary workers, and 1,000 contract workers, Kumar said. The management has also started issuing transfer orders to employees to shift to Bidadi plant near Bangalore without even discussing facilities like transport, he said.

The company's Bangalore plant has a history of workers' unrest, and the plant was shut down temporarily following a strike in September 2011.

Striking Bosch Workers in India Defy State Government Ban in October 2014

Striking Bosch workers at the Adugodi plant in Bangalore, southern India, are continuing a five-week strike for higher wages and better conditions, defying the outlawing of their strike by the Karnataka state government.

They are demanding a wage rise of at least 20%, the refund of wage cuts imposed on workers for earlier strikes, an end to harassment and the reinstatement of victimized workers. They are also fighting for permanency for temporary workers with more than 240 days' service, a halt to a Valid Time (VT) study, which aims to increase production targets, and the reversal of health scheme cuts.

In a blatant bid to break the strike on behalf of Bosch, the Congress party state government banned it on 10 October, invoking the 1947 Industrial Disputes Act. The company immediately demanded that workers end the strike, branding it 'illegal'. As a punitive measure, the company announced an eight-hour pay cut for every hour of striking.

On 14 October, Karnataka police arrested around 150 strikers when a thousand gathered in front of chief minister's residence to protest the government's ban. They were later released on bail.

German-based Bosch is one of the biggest automobile spare parts manufacturers in India. It has another plant in Bangalore—at Nagnathpura, on the state capital's outskirts—one at Nasik in Maharashtra, western India and one at Jaipur in Rajasthan, northern India. Bosch India, a major supplier to companies like Toyota and Maruti Suzuki, recorded a net profit of 8.85 billion rupees ($US308 million) in 2013 and 6.33 billion rupees in the first two quarters of this year.

Bosch's Adugodi plant has 2,300 permanent workers, 370 temporary workers, and 1,000 contract workers. On average, permanent workers are paid just 40,000 rupees ($649.3) a month. New entrant workers and temporary workers are paid about half that. Some young workers, employed as 'job trainees', get only 13,000 rupees per month, can be forced to work on all three shifts, and can be fired at any moment.

The company maintains this multi-tier workforce to divide workers and extract higher profits. But permanent, temporary, and contract workers have joined the strike, cutting across the management's attempt to split them. Workers have been denied a salary increment since it was due in January 2013. They rejected a management offer of a 5,500-rupee monthly rise, which does not cover the rising cost of living, and demanded an increase of 8,500 rupees.

When the WSWS interviewed strikers, one explained that the VT study aims to increase production targets to unreachable levels and thus abolish current incentives paid to workers. The management even removed seating arrangements for production workers, forcing them to stand, compromising their health.

Another striker denounced new limits imposed by the management on the medical reimbursement scheme. 'Every worker pays a monthly premium of 909 rupees for the medical reimbursement,' he explained. 'Now the compensation for major illness is limited at 150,000 rupees and compensation for serious illnesses like cancer is limited at 500,000 rupees.'

While the Bosch strikers are determined to fight, their union, the MEA, only reluctantly called the strike in the face of the mounting anger of workers. The union leaders have led workers on several marches to make appeals to the same government that has banned their strike.

In response to the 14 October arrests of strikers, MEA President Prasanna Kumar said: 'We went there to peacefully make our submissions to the chief minister and make him understand that the government's decision is in favour of management.' Even after the ban, the union is trying to promote illusions that the government can be convinced to support the strikers.

The MEA is working to isolate the strikers. It has not called on workers at the nearby Nagnathpura plant to join the strike, let alone other Bosch workers. It has made no appeal to workers in other industries. This flows from the politics of the MEA leaders.

President Kumar is associated with the Centre for Indian Trade Unions (CITU), affiliated to Stalinist Communist Party of India (Marxist) or CPM. The general secretary, Amarjeet Bhatia, who claims to be 'independent', is affiliated to the Industry All Global Union (IAGU). Other office bearers are associated with the Indian Trade Union Congress (INTUC), the union wing of Congress, which holds office in Karnataka and led the previous national government for 10 years.

The CITU and CPM have a long record of politically subordinating the working class to the capitalist parties, from Congress to various regional and caste-based parties. CPM is committed to defending the interests of local and foreign investors against workers and rural toilers, as was seen in West Bengal, where it led the Left Front government in West Bengal for 34 years until 2011.

Congress, the traditional party of the Indian bourgeoisie, initiated the pro-investor economic agenda in 1991, with devastating consequences for working people, and ruthlessly pursued those policies in the office from 1991 to 1996 and from 2004 to last May.

As for the IAGU, like all international trade unions, it functions on behalf of major corporations to suppress industrial action. In a 5 October letter to the IAGU, MEA General Secretary Bhatia said he had urged Bosch 'to urgently conduct an audit at Bosch Adugodi plant in connection with human rights violations, unfair labour practices, un-ergonomic work practices, inhuman working environment, compression work culture and other malpractices.' Bhatia asked for an opportunity for the MEA to meet with a member of Bosch's board.

Far from there being any differences between Bosch's Indian branch and its parent company in Germany, the appalling working conditions in Adugodi plant are driven directly by the profit interests of the German-based company.

More than 2,575 workers at the plant in Adugodi in the city went on strike on 16 September at the end of the legally stipulated notice period, demanding a new wage agreement to replace the one that lapsed in December 2012.

Although the gap between what the company was willing to give the workers and what the workers were willing to settle for appeared to be narrow, the difference was 'a matter of principle', said S. Prasanna Kumar, MICO Employees Association (Bosch's Indian subsidiary was earlier known as Motor Industries Company Ltd, or MICO). The two main unresolved issues pertain to medical benefits and the manner in which labour productivity is calculated. Prasanna Kumar said a solution to the question of medical benefits seemed imminent, but the company's position on labour productivity—and hence workers' wages—was characterized by 'ambiguity'.

Prasanna Kumar, also a general secretary of the Centre of Indian Trade Unions (CITU), said labour productivity should be based on a scientific study of time and motion of man and machine on the shop floor. He also said that although the existing productivity levels at the Adugodi plant were higher than those based on scientific norms, the company was unwilling to accept this and reward the workers. 'The company's stand is not based on any scientific principle, nor does it comply with any standardised productivity measure,' he claimed. He added that although the difference between the two sides, in financial terms, appeared to be only a few thousand rupees, the company's 'unwillingness to protect the workers' existing wages (achieved through higher productivity) reflects a stubborn and intransigent position that has no basis in any scientific method'.

Although the Karnataka Labour Department initiated talks on 18 September, it failed to break the deadlock. The company appealed for an 'adjudication process', implying that the dispute be resolved through a judicial process, which the union rejected. The union pointed out that allowing an already delayed wage settlement to pass through such a tortuous process was not only illogical but bad in law.

Ironically, the prolonged slowdown in the Indian automotive industry, which resulted in the pile-up of inventory levels, may be favourable to Bosch as it engages in a tussle with its workforce. But, clearly, recurring disputes with its workforce do not augur well for a company that likes to project itself as an 'ideal' employer.

Although the dispute veered towards a settlement in the second week of the strike, following the narrowing of the gap between the two sides, the union leadership is clear in its understanding that the question of the imbalance between the increase in productivity that workers deliver and the wages they earn remains a 'fundamentally unresolved question'. 'But that is a longer and wider battle, which we will continue to fight,' said Prasanna Kumar.

The 62-day ongoing strike has led to an estimated loss of around 2% of overall turnover registered during the period of the agitation.

Multinational engineering firm Bosch isn't really unfamiliar with labour trouble when it comes to its operations in India. But the ongoing 62-day strike at its biggest plant in the country, in Bangalore, is turning out to be one of the most protracted standoffs between the company and its workers in recent years.

The labour-related woes faced by the German company in Bangalore come in the midst of ambitious 'Make in India' campaign, which aims to put Indian manufacturing on the global map. Bosch's experience of dealing with its Indian workforce may put off potential global investors. It prompted the company's global chairman Volkmar Denner to comment, during his recent India visit, that repeated labour trouble could make Indian manufacturing uncompetitive.

Unlike the two relatively shorter 'tool-down' strikes that Bosch's Bangalore plant witnessed in 2013, the current one has been prohibited by the Karnataka government after conciliatory talks mediated by the state's labour department failed about a month ago. The Bosch workers' union, called MEA, challenged that order in the Karnataka High Court which gave the management and the union a chance to resolve the issue bilaterally. As no settlement was reached, the court will now take up the matter for hearing.

So far, the strike has led to an estimated loss of around 2% of overall turnover registered during the period of the agitation that started on 16 September. But it hasn't hurt the company's July–September quarter earnings in which Bosch posted a net profit of Rs 306.7 crore, a year-on-year increase of 30.8%. This was largely helped by an increase in non-operating income from the sale of some marketable securities. 'It (strike) will have some minor effect in the performance in the subsequent quarter. We are keen to resolve the issues with our union as we look forward to sustaining our growth and competitiveness in the market,' said Steffen Berns, managing director, Bosch Ltd.

Bosch Group in India generated sales of Rs 13,200 crore in the year ended 31 December, 2013. Bosch Ltd, the flagship company of the group in India, posted a profit after tax of Rs 885 crore, on net sales of Rs 8,641 crore in 2013. India is also home to Bosch's largest R&D centre outside Germany with around 10,500 engineers. According to Berns, the number of patents filed from the centre has grown more than tenfold to 220 patents last year from around 20 registered innovations in 2008.

The labour trouble at Bosch's Bangalore plant, formerly known as Motor Industries Co, which makes diesel pumps and common rail systems for vehicles, comes at a time when the auto industry has been going through a rough patch and may not have as adverse an impact on the firm as it could have otherwise. Declining auto sales has taken a toll on the auto ancillary sector as well. In fiscal 2014, the turnover of India's auto component industry declined 2% to Rs 2,11,765 crore ($35.13 billion). Several manufacturers including Bosch had to declare no-production days at their plants to prevent inventory pile-up.

Conclusions

Bosch was facing a lot of employee-related problems which ultimately turned into strike and lockout situations. And this situation repeats very often and has become a characteristic feature at many MNCs in spite of their presence in India over decades.

It is commonly felt that there is mostly the high-handed approach of the management in dealing with the internal environment at times succumbing also to these pressures gives rise to uncertain and disturbed relations between the management and the employees.

Case Questions

1. Explain the different strategies used by company to deal with strike and lockout situations.

2. How company was able to earn profit despite of all industrial relation issues?

3. What strategies are used by employees union to put forth their demand?

4. It appears that in general MNCs having their manufacturing units in India have frequent IR issues due at times to the operating culture in Indian and foreign companies and issues get to the brim quite often. How should such units have a cohesive approach without affecting operational efficiency?

2

Tata's Air India 'Take Over to Take Off'—A Cultural Conundrum

A Case Study on Tata's Takeover and Turnaround Strategy for Air India faced with Major Issues in Cultural Integration

Learning Objectives

This case study provides major insights to students and faculty in understanding concepts and major issues on cultural integration in mergers and takeovers especially in such cases of the government's disinvestment plans and uniquely the new buyer was a last owner 75 years ago of the same entity. From being a public sector unit to shift over to private sector ownership the employees will pose major issues in cultural transformation in their roles. Even students of Strategy Management, Human Resources Management, and executives involved in strategic integration will find this case study very interesting since it is a case study of the happening currently.

Synopsis

For N Chandrasekaran, newly appointed chairman of Tata's Air India, the aviation business has always been a nightmare. With Air India's CEO designate İlker Ayci out of the picture, Chandrasekaran's search for talent has become tougher. He may have to invest disproportionate time to the aviation vertical to turn around Air India and other loss-making airlines.

Indian Business Case Studies. V P Pawar, Bhagyashree Kunte, and Srinivas Tumuluri, Oxford University Press.
© ASM Group of Institutes, Pune, India 2022. DOI: 10.1093/oso/9780192869388.003.0002

Case Details

In one of the meeting rooms of the four-storey building, originally designed by famous Scottish architect George Wittet, a team of senior Tata Sons' executives were waiting for their boss, 'Chandra'. Phee Teik Yeoh the former Vistara CEO was expected to make a presentation on the state of the four-year-old airline start-up, a joint venture between Tata Sons' and its old-time partner Singapore Airlines, which was guzzling money.

For Chandrasekaran, who had joined Tata Consultancy Services (TCS) back in 1987 as a tech intern and climbed up the ladder to lead the group's crown jewel before taking over the reins of Tata Sons, aviation business has been a relative nightmare. Though the IT giant that churns out around INR40,000 crore in net profit every year provides software support to airlines across the globe, it did not change Chandrasekaran's view.

'He was not excited by aviation. He often used to repeat that in aviation, everyone makes money but for the airline,' a person who has worked with Chandrasekaran tells ET Prime, requesting anonymity.

When it comes to laying the foundation of airline operations of entities owned by Tata Sons, Chandrasekaran banks on experience from his TCS days. For example, he used to be a big fan of Norwegian Air. 'He personally knew the CEO of Norwegian Air and had told the Singaporeans at the 2017 meeting in Bombay House to benchmark Vistara with the former,' this person recalls, adding, 'The Singaporeans didn't like it at all.'

The nearly 50-year-old full-service Singapore Airlines sees itself as the benchmark in airline-service standards globally, while Norwegian Air, which was founded in 1993, is a budget airline with trailblazing expansion in transatlantic flights to its credit.

The Hunt for Talent (Change of Guards)

With former Turkish Airlines chairman and Air India's CEO designate İlker Ayci not joining the Tata Sons-owned airline, Chandrasekaran's search for the right talent has just got tougher.

Conversations with around two dozen officials involved in the Air India resurrection indicate that the first few weeks since the acquisition of the state-owned carrier by Tata Sons have not gone entirely as they would have liked them to go. And while there have been some changes, there is still a fog over the airline's medium- and long-term strategic direction.

The delay in the strategic and back-end reforms is partly because Chandrasekaran wanted to first appoint a CEO who could broadly run the day-to-day operations of the carrier, build its top management team, and recommend decisions like the merger among existing airlines, etc.

Hence, Tatas started the hunt for a CEO immediately after winning the bid to acquire Air India in October last year. A Zurich-based management consulting and executive search firm Egon Zehnder was given the task of finding the top five CEO candidates for Air India. Finding the right candidate turned out to be difficult as many ex-pat CEOs were not willing to relocate away from their families amid the pandemic.

Chandrasekaran, according to those who have worked with him, usually has a keen eye for getting the right talent. For example, in 2018 he had approved the appointment of Tata Steel's government affairs chief in Jamshedpur, Sunil Bhaskaran, as Air Asia India's CEO even though he had no experience in aviation.

Last year, Chandrasekaran tasked Tata Sons' group chief financial officer Saurabh Agrawal's close confidant and Tata Sons' Senior Vice-president Nipun Aggarwal with leading the bidding for Air India. Aggarwal didn't disappoint and Tatas acquired Air India with little debt (the government has taken over most of it and allocated INR52,000 crore in next year's budget for the same), though with some handicaps.

'Nipun is very aggressive in the way he talks. He is an investment banker who cuts deals, so he has an aggressive stance,' says a third person, who knows Aggarwal well, requesting anonymity. 'If you say you will revert on something by tomorrow, he will tell you—"in one hour, get it done".'

For the Air India CEO role though Ayci seems to have made the cut. He resigned from Turkish Airlines' board the day Tata Sons won Air India. Chandrasekaran was very keen to rope in Ayci despite his close ties with Erdogan, who is not seen as an India-friendly leader, and alleged links to an al-Qaida financier. Partly, the confidence of securing the Indian government's clearance for the appointment of Ayci may have stemmed from a recent experience. Tata's air-conditioner maker Voltas and Turkey's household appliances manufacturer Arcelik had joined hands in 2017 to expand the consumer durables sector in India and that venture had gone forward without any challenges.

But aviation is different. Behind the scenes, some union members of Air India were worried about Ayci's tough stance towards labour unions. Hence, they kept on bringing up his appointment at Air India as a security risk. These unions typically also reach out to various political outfits. Days after Ayci's name was announced, some of the critics went public saying the government should not give security clearance to Ayci 'keeping in view national security'.

(While TCS is known for excellent due diligence on the global contracts it signs, it's quite clear that someone was caught sleeping at the wheel as Tatas couldn't foresee this despite appointing a top CEO-search firm like Zehnder. A quick background check on another Turkish firm may have helped. Turkey-originated ground-handling firm Celebi, which operates at Indian airports, has had to often emphasise that it is mostly backed by US-based investors).

Typically, it takes around three-four months for foreign nationals to get security clearance from India's home ministry while resident Indians such as Chandrasekaran get it in a month or two. It is unlikely that Chandrasekaran would have waited for the incoming CEO to give the airline strategic direction if his entry into India would have taken six months or even more.

Further checks made by ET Prime showed that Tatas had applied for security clearance for Chandrasekaran besides Hindustan Unilever's chairman and managing director Sanjiv Mehta, to be appointed on Air India's board on 11 February. Three days later, Ayci's name was announced for the CEO's post. But his papers were not moved for security clearance. Two weeks since, he 'declined' the role citing controversy.

'They spent the last 20 days to convince the man to ease out of this given the situation,' says a person aware of the subject. 'He would have even got the security clearance, but with this baggage of stories he may have found it difficult to work in the system. The very fact that Tatas have not sent his papers for security clearance shows that there was a rethink.'

It appears that Tata's are again looking for an ex-pat CEO and is hoping to make an announcement in the next few weeks.

As the search for the new CEO is still underway, the airline has chosen to focus on the low-hanging fruit.

The Attitudinal Change

Over the past few weeks, Air India has seen an improvement in its on-time flight performance at metros which is now touching around 95%.

So, how was this achieved?

To begin with, Tata Sons has been looking into the processes at Air India since December last year, another person aware of the subject, who did want to be named, points out. The group found that the airline did not monitor on-time performance on the same day as the reports used to come only the next day. This has changed. There is also a new mechanism to ensure regional directors are in touch with each other more often.

Further, the airline's pilots sometimes used to release the parking brakes of their aircraft even without clearance from the air traffic control (ATC) to push back. This was sometimes done for technical reasons, but it often allowed pilots to clock in more payable work hours and was hurting the airline. A change in this process alone has improved Air India's on-time performance by around 0.5%.

Since the new management wants to ensure that flights are on schedule, the pilots are also pushing the crew members to close the gates on time before take-off. For instance, the first flight of the day, say at around 5 am, is being strictly monitored and the gates are to be closed 20 minutes before the departure. If the first departure happens on time, there is also some buffer time for any delays throughout the day.

Some pilots used to swing by the Starbucks outlets to grab a cup of coffee even at the cost of delaying their flights, or even held up flights if they were not picked up on time by the company's transport, 'The change in attitude, however, has happened only for 20% of the employees. That's because they are scared of losing their jobs. For the majority, the attitude shift has not happened yet.'

As per the privatization agreement, Tatas cannot terminate Air India staff for one year. This means the airline's employees have got roughly 10 more months to prove their merit. The Tatas are also considering bringing in a voluntary retirement scheme (VRS) for its employees, the second official says. And while that VRS can be brought even now, the government has asked the group to avoid it for a year.

Knowing the challenges that come with transitioning an airline, which was run ad-hoc under the 'guidance', earlier Chandrasekaran has entrusted Tata Steel's former human resources head Suresh Tripathi with the job.

Tripathi has started a video-conferencing session called #Takeoff, in which employees can share their problems and in turn get to hear the updates on airline's future plans. Apart from this, they have been given an e-mail address to send their problems. Queries are run through various departments and replied to. In these sessions, Tripathi, who has handled labour unions in the past, has been both empathetic and stern. He has clearly conveyed to the employees that promotions will be purely on merit going forward.

When pilots asked about salary hikes, Tripathi was blunt. 'First, we need to make money to give it to the employees. So, for first year, the priority is to streamline the airline,' he told them, according to the fifth person quoted above.

Service Standards

Another area of focus at the airline is on improving service standards and its crew members are required to attend a two-day refresher course.

During onboarding announcements, passengers are now addressed as 'guests', and in Hindi, *yatriyon* (passengers) has become *athithis* (guests), reflecting this change.

The crew has also been asked to stop addressing each other as 'sir' or 'madam', and use first names instead. This has not gone down well with the senior crew members.

Further, there is also a gap in expectation from the crew and what is actually being supplied on domestic flights.

For example, passengers are to be given hot and cold towels, but that is not happening in some flights. While breadbasket has been brought back, the tongs to serve bread are sometimes not available and there is often no silver entrée to serve juices.

'The training is designed in a very hasty way. It's more for wide-body cabin crew but even narrow-body crew has to do it,' says an old official.

Many members of the wide-body crew are also unhappy that the airline has decided that everyone will be cross-trained on all fleet types. Some see it as a demotion to serve narrow-body planes. Since the Indian Airlines and Air India merger, the airline has continued to function as two separate entities in many ways—narrow body and wide body. While ideally this aircraft cross-training should have been done long back to save costs and improve flight operations, the training is yet to start even now.

Historically, Air India has not pushed its crew to shed bodyweight because of the strong stand taken by the union. While weight checks were done for the crew only during the medical examination, which typically was once in four years, compared with Vistara's monthly checks, even when the crew were caught on the higher side they were given warning and asked to reduce weight within a certain time. This deadline was often extended as well.

Now, though grooming associates have been hired internally to have these checks more often, they have been only collecting data so far. If they penalize crew members who are overweight, then it becomes the new Air India. Otherwise, it's the same old airline opines an observer.

Inflight Refreshments

In its bid to makeover the airline's image, Tatas have been magnanimous in overhauling the menu even though the cost recovery may be difficult. A plain coleslaw sandwich has given way to a corn-cheese sandwich, while instead of a small Dairy Milk chocolate, a *kheer chamcham* is served as dessert.

'There is the same coterie that is still operating in the crew department and there are so many skeletons. Nothing will change. Infusing fresh talent is very critical. They should get someone with vast experience in managing full-service airlines to head this department first,' says a person with direct knowledge of the subject.

The Urgent Renovations

The Legacy

The persistent cash crunch has also been a drag on Air India. For example, the airline does not have the kind of forecasting tools that are needed to gauge demand, analyse historical trends, and manage its pricing accordingly. Air India has also not been able to upgrade its crew rostering and dispatcher software. 'Forget software, we don't even have laptops. Only some seniors have them. If we buy new software, our computers will surely crash,' says an erstwhile employee official.

However, Tatas have been prompt in whitewashing Air India's offices and introducing regular cleaning of the buildings and premises besides ensuring that salaries are paid on time. TCS executives have also been stationed at the Air India office to collect detailed data on revenue management and other domains. TCS will also have to create hundreds of new company e-mail addresses as Tatas have found, according to the second official, that many employees simply use Gmail/Hotmail/Yahoo, etc. for official purpose.

'From the perspective of customer service, the focus of the organisation is now on enhancing overall customer experience at all the touch points. Towards this objective, a total revamp of process and procedure is underway with the sole mission to provide a quick resolution to passenger issues,' Air India spokesman adds.

A Major Handicap

Engineering Services

While Chandrasekaran may have cut a good deal on Air India, Tata got the airline minus the critical engineering department, which is a different subsidiary under government control.

'It's a huge vulnerability,' says an official, adding, 'How does one order around someone who is not in your control but can impact your flight operations and aircraft turnaround time?'

Indeed, some of the employees of AI Engineering Services Ltd (AIESL) have gone on strike this week citing poor remuneration and this has disrupted a few flights. While AIESL will continue to serve Air India, its legacy contracts are also 30% more expensive than what it would have cost if it was being done internally like other airlines, says a ninth official aware of the contracts.

Mounting Operational Losses

Besides engineering services, Chandrasekaran will also have to deal with Air India's losses, which aren't likely to go away soon. The airline is likely to report a net loss of around INR5,000 crore in FY22 and could make a similar or even bigger loss in the next fiscal because of a fleet upgrade plan, a potential aircraft order, and higher oil prices.

This is after taking into account the reduced interest burden as most of Air India's debt has been taken over by the government and the fact that the airline will now get small advantages such as fuel discounts from the likes of Indian Oil for paying its bills on time and has already got better terms on loans from lenders such as the State Bank of India.

While Chandrasekaran is known to give plenty of freedom to the top management of group companies, he wants to see return on cost of capital and doesn't shy away from shuffling the team if it doesn't perform.

In the group's loss-making airlines, Vistara and AirAsia India, Chandrasekaran has been potentially restrained as they are international joint ventures where initially only functions such as finance and human resource were allotted to the Tatas

To Agrawal's dismay, their pitches would be followed by even more aggressive expansion plans for their airlines. And that's when Chandrasekaran would intervene and say 'Let's not try to be over-ambitious, but rather improve things on a year-on-year basis. We can't become IndiGo overnight. We need to first become number #2 or number #3.'

With Air India in its portfolio, however, Tatas are already number #2 in domestic aviation market share now and number #1 when it comes to international market share. But to reach IndiGo's pre-pandemic profits, Chandrasekaran will take time which is going to be very challenging

Conclusions

The case study is very current and the student's faculty needs to follow-up each milestone which Tatas need to cross over to make the take over a grand success as envisaged by the current chairman Mr N

Chandrasekharan and also to full fill long-cherished sentimental dream project of Mr Ratan Tata the Iconic Leader of Tatas.

Case Questions

1. Do you think Tatas overall approach to take over (buyback) of Air India which some seven decades ago was a part of Tatas Crown jewel mostly a decision based on business sentiments? What is the rationale behind when the aviation industry has a rough weather for some time?

2. What according to you are the major hurdles which Tatas will face in resurrecting Air India and integrating in to Tata Group?

3. What important analysis and steps/strategies you suggest Tatas should follow to make Air India prosper under Tata brand?

3

Beyond the Bootstrap

A Case of Sophisticated Entrepreneur

Learning Objectives

To understand the nature of entrepreneurship as entrepreneurs are competitive and always strive to gain an edge over their competitors. To study the entrepreneurial business ideas and identify personal attributes of the employees that enable the best use of entrepreneurial opportunities. Explore entrepreneurial leadership and management style. To study how business situations consist of real challenges, constraints, and opportunities that directly impact on the business performance of a firm.

Synopsis

This case is about entrepreneurial capabilities and attitudinal aspects as important to manage situations in a competitive marketplace. The first-time entrepreneurs are normally experienced and trained in manufacturing and management skills before they decide to start their own enterprises.

Whereas in case of entrepreneurs who take up responsibilities as entrepreneurs in a family succession plan it becomes challenging to manage enterprises which have already got used to a set culture and management styles and difficult to deviate and change to corner room management styles. The second-generation entrepreneurs are not easily accepted by the workforce and group dynamics established from the past periods.

Normally the second-generation entrepreneurs are more exposed to lifestyles and attitudes of highly educated and convent bread styles of life.

Indian Business Case Studies. V P Pawar, Bhagyashree Kunte, and Srinivas Tumuluri, Oxford University Press.
© ASM Group of Institutes, Pune, India 2022. DOI: 10.1093/oso/9780192869388.003.0003

To work with own hands and be friendly and accommodative towards employees is not a simple possibility and leads to complex issues in managing the enterprise. The protagonist of the case apparently belongs to one such class of entrepreneur over dependent on his predecessors' generals.

Case Details: Kurlekar Precision Engineering Pvt Ltd

Rajendra Kurlekar, an entrepreneur by birth (nicknamed Rajan by his family members, and Dada Saheb to his employees), was angry and upset when his close friend and a fellow entrepreneur, Kishor Limaye, walked in to his office for the usual morning cup of tea and chat. Kishor Limaye could easily make out that something was seriously amiss and sensed the depressing vibes around him. He could clearly see that Rajan was highly distressed from his pinkish face. Kishor Limaye, therefore, decided to sidestep the usual greetings and enquiries about business issues; instead, he started by chiding the failure of the meteorological office, which was expected, and talking about the absence of rains leading to problems of water shortage in the industrial estate. Rajan, befitting his cosmopolitan behaviour, greeted Kishor Limaye with a tight—faced artificial smile; however, he soon fell back to his grim state of mind. The disturbed situation at his unit had been bothering Rajan since the previous evening. Kishor Limaye was one of Rajan's best friends, who provided Rajan shoulders to lean on whenever there was a disappointing situation, be it personal or official.

The case study explains the classic example of entrepreneurship.

Rajan had migrated to Pune, some 10 years ago when new Maharashtra Industrial Development Corporations (MIDCs) were being set up in and around Pune. Major industries such as the Tata, Thermax, Philips, and the Marshall group of industries were on their expansion modes. Since Rajan did not prefer to be away from the city of Pune, he had re-established his unit at MIDC, at Parvati Industrial Estate, under the new name 'Rajan Precision Engineering Pvt. Ltd'. Rajan belonged to a family of entrepreneurs; his father, late Chandrakant Kurlekar, was a well-known importer of precision machinery and spares from European countries, who had also established a small service set-up for imported machinery at Wadala, Mumbai, in the early 1970s. Rajan's brother, Vinay Kurlekar, was busy exploiting the contacts that their father had established over decades of follow-up work through the Director General of Supplies and Goods (DGS & D) and other government machinery for continuation of the import of machinery and spares. During the process, Vinay got in to representing foreign companies to Indian manufacturers, and eventually around the mid-1970s he shifted his base to Germany. In the process of importing machinery and spares, the Kurlekars attempted a vertical integration by importing certain crucial machines for the manufacture of precision components and subassemblies; they also started a small unit at their Wadala unit to directly cater to the requirements of such components by Philips India Marshalls Pvt Ltd, and other precision instrument manufacturers. This unit at Wadala-Mumbai thrived in the early1970s, but soon they had to think of shifting their unit outside Mumbai for logistics and cost reasons, besides focusing on further growth in their manufacturing business. And since the major customer base was in Pune, it was logical for them to shift to Pune in the mid-1980s.

Industry Shift from Mumbai to Pune

Rajan's initial stint in Mumbai enabled him to work on the business contacts established by his father. He also learnt his initial lessons in entrepreneurship from the management of his plant and machinery, from his father and the related issues in the management of raw materials, finances, and other regulatory requirements from the MIDC, etc., after he shifted to Pune. However, Rajan maintained his 'Superior cult' behaviour among his fellow industrialists in the MIDC Pune on account of his imported machines and his high-profile customer base, and in view of his specialized nature towards products. There were no competing units in and around Pune therefore, he was a preferred supplier of his buyers. This attitude, however, delineated Rajan from easy accessibility of otherwise conventional suppliers of tools and foundry products in the MIDC. Rajan also made sure that only a few of his trusted employees from the Mumbai unit shifted to Pune; even the administrative staff was transferred from the Mumbai operations. This arrangement, while ensuring continuity in operations and loyalty, created employee groups in the set-up between the ones transferred from Mumbai and the locally recruited staff and workers. Rajan cared more for those who had worked in Mumbai incidentally. This was because, with his brother Vinay severing his business involvement from the manufacturing unit, and with his father's demise in 1985, Rajan had to fend for the Mumbai unit entirely on his own.

In the initial period, the unit received only part of the orders for the requirements of its customers, since many-wanted Kurlekars' new unit at Pune to ensure the quality of its supplies and maintain schedules. Rajan was, however, able to establish confidence in his clients because of the loyalty and commitment he derived from his reliable employees who were transferred from Mumbai. And in a short period of six months, he was able to get repeat and bulk orders from his customers such as Philips India, Marshalls Pvt Ltd., and many more.

Internal Chaos and Consequences

Soon, around 1998, the going started getting tougher, since the old employees whom he had nursed carefully started complaining of family and other issues with few of them wanting to get back to Mumbai to attend to their elderly parents whom they had left behind while shifting to Pune. The newly employed engineers and supervisors also started feeling that there are inadequate career growth opportunities at Kurlekars' unit, resulting in lack of interest and motivation in their jobs from. During this period, Rajan had to frequently travel between Pune and Mumbai to arrange for the raw material requirements of his set-up and also to meet with his customers in other locations at Bengaluru, Kolkata, and Chennai. Rajan was also required to focus on his own family issues as his son Vivek needed to be sent abroad for higher studies and his daughter needed to secure admission in a local college for her graduation. His health also started posing problems on account of his inconsistent lifestyle and lack of respite from the escalating problems at his factory.

The resignations at the middle-management level and the growing groupism among the junior-level staff and some workers were creating major problems in maintaining quality and meeting the supply schedules of its customers. This led to heavy rejections of supplies by Philips, who needed supplies of high precision and quality for their final electronic products Philips India claimed collateral damages on Kurlekars for the increased customer complaints on their finished products. Continuation of this situation for a prolonged period resulted in the cancellation of orders from other customers as well. Delayed payments, the cost of rejections, and rework started straining the financial situation. As though the problems were not enough, the workers under the leadership of Anil Kamble (son of an old employee) formed a workers' union and started agitations against the management for wage negotiations and better working conditions in the factory. Rajan was also was dependent heavily on one Ramesh Purandare who was in charge of the tool design and development along with maintenance functions of high-precision imported machines. Purandare had worked previously with Kurlekars in their Mumbai unit. In view of Purandare's job-related importance and criticality of the functions he handled, Rajan used to deal directly on all matters related to Purandare and always made sure that Purandare was kept happy all the time. Purandare, on the other hand, was highly capable and did not tolerate anyone other than Rajan directly assigning him any task. He was extremely moody at times, which led to constant tiffs with the operations people. At times Purandare was very rude and uncompromising. He, on account of feeling indispensable and overconfident, used to drive the production supervisors, who were constantly under pressure from Rajan to maintain delivery schedules of customer orders to tears. During the frequent absences of Rajan on account of business travel, Purandare's stature grew bigger than Rajan's and he started dictating terms with one and all at the factory. Even though Rajan was aware of the situation created by Purandare, he was helpless and not able to talk directly to Purandare on this matter. He also knew that Purandare could walk over him to the competition along with a few of his trusted and highly skilled workers. Several times in the past, Kishore Limaye had advised Rajan to recruit a few fresh engineers to be trained under Purandare for future eventualities, including succession planning. Girish Abhyankar, Chirag Patne, and Umesh Kulkarni were a few who were recruited to achieve this objective. However, Purandare, who was himself a trained technician from ITI Ambernath, did not relish the idea of qualified engineers joining the organization, who would eventually become threats to the unquestioned power and authority that he had managed to acquire in the set-up.

Meanwhile, on account of the growth of markets, the competition to M/s Kurlekars became severe. In fact, a few of the ex-employees of Kurlekars had joined the company's competitors at higher salaries and positions and had started exposing the deficiencies of Kurlekars to the customers. In the past, Rajan had sent some of his efficient engineers to foreign exhibitions as a reward for their performance and potentials, but he lost the same employees to his competition mainly because of the non-congenial work atmosphere at Kurlekars.

Over the previous few months, Rajan was feeling very lonely and depressed; he lost sleep and started worrying over the problems that he was facing in his business. He started to frequently fall back on Kishor Limaye's advice, since he had lost faith in the senior-level executives of his factory. He felt that several of his managers were conspiring to create more trouble in his organization by colluding with some of his ex-employees who were now working for the competitors. The escalating labour issues also increased his anxiety. It was on a Wednesday afternoon, around 5 p.m., that Rajan, while on a business tour, received a frantic call from his shift manager informing that the workers at the factory had resorted to a lightning strike on account of an injury suffered by one of the workers while working on a machine, which had just in the previous shift, been attended by Purandare's team for break down repairs. To add insult to injury, there was a shortage of snacks in the canteen, as the contractor had failed to make the required quantity of food on account of power failure in the canteen. Apprehending a major clash with the workers led by their leader Kamble, the shift manager had asked the workers to go outside the factory gate, assuring them that the workers will be marked present for the whole shift and would not be penalized for their absence. The shift manager, however, had also telephoned the production in charge at his residence and kept him informed about the developments at the factory. Meanwhile, Rajan tried to contact Purandare to ask him as to how the accident had occurred on a freshly repaired machine. Sensing the intention of Rajan's call, Purandare who was on his way to Mumbai on a personal visit did not take the call. Understanding the gravity of the situation, Rajan decided to curtail his tour and returned to Pune by the next available flight.

He was also concerned about the communication from his plant head that the work on the shop floor is not likely to resume in the next two-to-three days due to the unavailability of critical raw materials that had not reached the factory due to the transport strike, which had started the same day midnight. Also, there was huge pile-up of rejections received back from the customers that needed rework, rectification, and sorting. Anand Bakshi from Philips India had summoned Rajan to visit them at the earliest to discuss major quality problems in the supplies.

On the advice of Kishor Limaye, Rajan telephoned Advocate Dinesh Dashrath, asking him to offer consultancy services to get over the current Industrial Relations (IR) issues and also to help in maintaining industrial peace and harmony in the organization.

As expected, Rajan rushed to the factory the next day morning at 7 a.m. sharp; he was highly disappointed to see workers of the first shift squatting outside the factory gate, trying to intimidate his entry with high-pitched slogans and criticisms against the management for the chaotic situation. As Rajan walked in, he saw that the shift-in-charge Patne was busy reading the morning newspaper and enjoying a hot cup of tea in his chair. Patne did not expect to see Rajan in the factory so early in the day; he left his tea halfway and rushed to greet Rajan. Rajan was furious that Patne appeared least worried about the current situation in the factory; he raised his voice and shouted at Patne as to how he could sit quiet when the workers had not resumed their work and were allowed to squat outside the gate shouting slogans against the management. Patne felt insulted, since he felt that there was hardly anything he could have done to make the agitated workers listen to him to resume work.

Rajan also telephoned Abhyankar, the production-in-charge, and instructed him to come over to the factory at the earliest, while requesting Dashrath the labour consultant to also come over for an urgent meeting on labour issues. Meanwhile, Patne gathered courage to explain to Rajan the sequence of events that had occurred around 6.30 a.m., the starting time for the first shift on that day. He explained that although a few workers had come inside the factory after punching their attendance, Kamble, the union leader had come in and asked these workers not to start work. Kamble came over to Patne who was busy assigning jobs to various machines based on the plan. Kamble snatched the planning sheet from Patne's hands and threw it in the dustbin; he warned Patne that no worker should be asked to work till the grievances of the workers were resolved. He also accused Patne of ignoring the safety of the workers and also being casual about tea and snacks from the canteen, which were far below the quality levels and caused dysentery and other stomach ailments to the workers. All the workers joined Kamble and started pushing Patne from his chair till he fell down on the floor. Patne got irritated due to this manhandling by the workers he got up and slapped Kamble in the face and asked him and the other workers to leave the factory premises forthwith. He also asked the security to drive out the slogan-shouting workers.

Rajan huddled in his cabin with Abhyankar, Patne, and Dashrath. He also tried to call Purandare for a teleconference, but he was upset to note that Purandare had left Mumbai on his way to Nasik with his family for a pilgrimage and was not reachable for the next three/four days.

In the meeting, Patne restated the ugly incidences that had taken place at the start of the first shift on that day and defended his actions as the situation had gone out of hand. Abhyankar explained that the trouble had started in the second shift of previous day; he had been apprehensive of some likely accident since, according to him, Purandare's team did not carefully attend the particular machine. Abhyankar had been asked by Purandare not to talk about machine-related issues about which he had no knowledge or experience. He also instructed the shift supervisor to start regular production on the repaired machine disregarding the apprehensions of Abhyankar.

While the meeting was in progress, the receptionist informed Rajan over the intercom that Kamble had sent a message through the security that he, along with an outside leader and a few workers, wanted to meet Rajan urgently, and if their request for the meeting was refused they would not be responsible for the consequences and damages, if any, to company vehicles; they also threatened to put on fire the entire premises of the factory. Rajan took Dashrath to a corner, explained to him the matter that he had heard on the telecom and asked his opinion as to how to react or respond to the union's demand. Dashrath, who was by then fairly clear about the issues, advised Rajan to meet the union leaders in an adjoining room, while he would have further discussions with Abhyankar and Patne.

Rajan accordingly asked the receptionist to send the union leaders to a separate room adjoining his cabin immediately. Kamble along with the outside leader and two of the senior workers came in to meet Rajan (all had tied red bands on their foreheads as a sign of protest), and handed over to Rajan an envelope containing the demands of their union. They informed Rajan that unless their demands were met none of the workers would resume work at the factory, and further demanded an immediate payment of Rs 10,000 for the urgent treatment of the workman who had been injured in the previous shift. They further explained that Patne and Rajan should apologize for the slap given to Kamble by Patne. They left the meeting, shouting, and abusing Patne and threatening him physical harm outside the factory premises if he did not apologize personally to Kamble, the union leader. Rajan asked the union leaders to mind their words and not to resort to any hooliganism in and around the factory premises. Rajan again called Dashrath separately and explained the demands letter from the union and their threats to manhandle Patne. Dashrath called for the personal files of Kamble and the two other senior workers who had come in to meet Rajan, went through them and dictated a suspension-pending-enquiry notice in their names. He advised Rajan to sign these orders of suspension and issue them to the concerned workers. Dashrath left the meeting asking Rajan to keep him updated on the day-to-day developments in the labour situation. Rajan continued with his discussions with Abhyankar and Patne, but, they were not able to arrive at any definite line of action. Rajan had not forgotten the summons he had received from Bakshi of Philips India he was worried about his not having any immediate assurances to give to Bakshi on the quality issues He felt like everyone around him was intimidating him and no one was ready to take major responsibility in restoring normalcy in the operations at the factory. Kishor Limaye, who had come to talk over certain issues, found Rajan in a disturbed mood that had never been so apparent in past.

Conclusions

Vibrant entrepreneurship requires support from an enabling ecosystem of culture, finance, expertise, infrastructure, skills, and business-friendly regulation.

Personal and business motivations, peer pressures, and cultural influences also influence business perceptions. The entrepreneur should avoid these mistakes while building the team—not treating each team member as an individual, using only financial motivation, not sharing your long-term vision, shying away from tough conversations, not delegating enough are the main obstacles in the smooth management of entrepreneurial ventures.

Case Questions

1. What strategy should be applied by Rajan while assigning the change to Purandare keeping in mind about the criticality of the current situation of his firm shifting from Mumbai to Pune?

2. Do you think that profit maximization is the main motivation of the Rajan as an entrepreneur?

3. Comment on the points to be considered before expecting the teamwork from member of organizations at every level. Which area of the labour laws has to be emphasized more during development of successful business model in organization?

4. Does profit have to be the main motivation of a successful business owner?

5. Which are the salient strategic issues that in your view needed to be focused upon by Kurlekars before and immediately after shifting their operations to Pune?

4

Starbucks—The 'Coffee House' Experts

A Case Study in Cultural and Strategic Alignment

Learning Objectives

The learning objectives of this case study are firstly, to understand the historical background of Starbucks, secondly, to learn about their methods of motivating employees, and thirdly, to study the strategies used by them to enhance the work performance of their employees.

Synopsis

Because of rapid globalization over recent years, the competition around the world becomes, more intense, especially for the service industry with similar products. The most critical point for business to succeed is not only the quality of products they supply, but the atmosphere of cooperating and the amount that teamwork yields in retail sales. The employees who always touch with customers and can realize what customers really need are first-line staff. Therefore, it is essential for companies to motivate, reward, and train their employees to be the best quality personnel. Starbucks Corporation, the most famous chain of retail coffee shops in the world, mainly benefits from roasting, selling special coffee beans and various kinds of coffee or tea drinks. It owns about 4000 branches in the whole world. Moreover, it has been one of the most rapid growing corporations in America as well. The reasons why Starbucks is popular worldwide are not only the quality of coffee, but also its customer service and cosy environment. Starbucks

Indian Business Case Studies. V P Pawar, Bhagyashree Kunte, and Srinivas Tumuluri, Oxford University Press.
© ASM Group of Institutes, Pune, India 2022. DOI: 10.1093/oso/9780192869388.003.0004

establishes comfortable surroundings for people to socialize with a fair price, which attracts all age ranges of consumers to get into the stores. Besides, it is also noted for its satisfaction of employees. The turnover rate of employees at Starbucks was 65% and the turnover rate of managers was 25% a year. However, the rates of other national chain retailers are 150% to 400% and 50% respectively. Compared with them, the turnover rate of Starbucks is much lower than other industries on an average. As a result, Starbucks would be one of the optimal business models for understanding the strategies of employee motivation, customer satisfaction, and cooperation of teamwork.

The History of Starbucks

Starbucks was formed by three friends, Jerry Baldwin, Zev Siegl, and Gordon Bowker, who knew each other at the University of Seattle. In 1971, their first store named 'Starbucks Coffee, Tea, and Spice' was set up in Seattle, Washington's Pike Place Market. They engaged in making profit from selling coffee and roasted beans to individual customers and restaurants. Until 1982, they had increased the number of stores to four. During the same period, a sales representative of the houseware business in New York, Hammerplast, visited them. Howard Schultz wanted to know why a small company needs a large number of percolators from Hammerplast. Because of the trade relationship between these two companies, he was acquainted with the three inventors. After he realized the atmosphere and environment of the company, he decided to be a part of Starbucks, then as a director of marketing and retail sales. In the following year, he had a vacation in Milan, Italy. Throughout the time, he experienced an entirely different coffee culture from the United States. The culture of Italian café had been one part of peoples' daily life. There were numerous coffee bars around the area and the public usually liked to socialize in a coffee bar. Under those circumstances, Schultz had an idea of a new flavour of café and a stylish environment to communicate with friends.

After the trip, he prepared the business plan for his vision. However, the three initiators did not want to transfer their business into restaurant industry. Consequently, in 1985 he chose to establish a new coffee shop, named II Giornale, in Seattle. After the next two years, due to the successful strategy of Schultz, the original three owners of Starbucks decided to sell their corporation to Schultz. Then Schultz gathered other investors and took over the name of II Giornale to Starbucks. He sought to pursue his dream to make everyone taste his coffee, so he focused on the rate of expanding. At that time, he thought that the most efficient way to grow the amount of branches was to set up new stores in other places. In 1987, Starbucks had the first overseas store in Japan. In the subsequent years, owing to the rising expenses with the worldwide broadening, there was a deficit in Starbucks for the next three years. In contrast, he firmly believed not to 'sacrifice long-term integrity and values for short-term profit'. In 1991, it turned around from a loss to gain and its sales grew up sharply to 84%. Until the end of 2002, Starbucks had developed from 17 stores to 5,688 stores spreading over 30 countries. It was an over 300 times growth in these ten years! Fortune magazine ranked Starbucks as the 26th best company to work for in 2005, in the USA which then rose to 11th in 2006. In 2007, it was ranked as the 16th best. In the same year, Starbucks was also voted as one of the top ten UK workplaces by the financial times.

Motivation

Motivation is a vital factor for this business during the process of making their production. Labours are not working machines and cannot always do the same work with equal passion. Accordingly, an efficient method to keep the staff keen on their jobs would be to motivate them. It might even gain a better yield than purchasing plenty of equipment and facilities. However, contrary to the classical management approaches, some reports had proposed that the ways to motivate employees are not only money. Kohn showed a survey that if companies offer only physical rewards, the produce from workers might decline, especially in the creativity industries. Other factors are essential as well, such as working environment or relationship between employees and managers.

Nicholson reported that 'workers had strong social needs which they tried to satisfy through membership of informal social groups at work place'. Besides, 'the importance of informal social factors in the work place such as co-worker relationships and group norms that influence employee motivation and performance is highlighted'.

A previous researcher, Pugh and Hickson cited Elton Mayo who made an investigation called the 'Hawthorne Experiment'. According to the results, if managers provided a suitable working environment considering each personal requirement and their sense of satisfaction rather than a higher salary or bonus, workers were encouraged to be more hardworking and efficient. He also verified that if managers of an organization do not consider individual worker's needs and wants and treat them as equal units, this would 'maximize payment and minimize effort'. As a result, how to use non-financial incentives would be an important issue for business nowadays.

The chief executive officer of Starbucks corporation, Howard Schultz, considers that the tip of success in Starbucks is not coffee but employees. Constantly accumulating the working experience of employees and providing chances of promotion in a company for working partners is the way to operate sustainability. He firmly believes that the spirit of Starbucks is employed and feels honoured about the value of Starbucks employees. For this reason, it is necessary to have a perfect education and training policy for better performance in a company (Michelli, 2006). Starbucks offers an interactive structure that makes personnel dedicate themselves to their job. They motivate their partners to satisfy themselves, achieving a new level of performance.

Equal Treatment

The managers in Starbucks treat each staff member equally and all of the staff members are called partners, even the supervisors of each branch are called so as well. In order to narrow the gap between managers and employees, they also co-work with the basic level staffs in the front line. Due to this, they can maintain a well-honed management system and create a much closer and more familiar atmosphere than other places. This not only makes employees enjoy their job but also customers are positively affected by their enthusiasm.

Listen to Employees

Starbucks has a well-organized communication channel for employees. It places a great importance on labours. For example, managers plan the working hours per worker and arrange the schedule of time off, according to their wants, to meet their requirements. There are weekly interviews to see what the employees' needs are. A special survey called Partner View Survey is taken, approximately in every two years. The managers can receive feedbacks through the event to understand which part should be improved or what issue should be paid more attention to. The partners have the right to figure out what is the best policy for them, and the directors show respect for each suggestion. Starbucks even wants every employee to join in making and developing plans, then achieving their goals all together. As a result, the policies and principles are communicated between all staff, and there is no limitation to employees' personal opinions. This way the business can improve their strategies and even innovate through different ideas.

Good Welfare Measures

All employees, including informal personnel, are offered a great deal of welfare policies, for instance, commodities discounts for employees, medical insurance (including health, vision, and dental), and vacations. Moreover, the partners who work over 20 hours a week are entitled for benefits. Starbucks also thinks that debt financing is not the best choice, thus it chose a stock dividend option to all employees with a free scrip issue. By this policy, the employees can get benefits from the dividends of the company. Because of this, they have the same goal; in other words, they are motivated to increase the sales to earn more profits. Starbucks just handles personnel with its core value, which is, 'employees are the most important asset of Starbucks'. Showing respect to employees and well-developed environment have led Starbucks to produce the best work environment for employees and an increase in profits.

Teamwork

Teamwork can construct not only a small social structure in organization for employees to socialize, but also a composite of various kind of members who are equipped with different backgrounds of skill and knowledge on account of the mission. Each member plays an important role in the teamwork; therefore everyone in that team can meet their needs for getting acquainted with different colleagues and also learn new skills from each other. Hoegl and Gemuenden observed that the definition of teamwork is a social system including more than three people in an organization or context. These members identify others as one member of the team and they have the same goal. Robbins stated that the factors influencing teamwork are relation of leadership, roles, principles, status, size, composition, and the power of agglomerate.

The Strategies to Keep Well Relationship

Starbucks establishes a well-developed system to keep good relationship between managers and employees. At first, the leaders of retail shops use the same title 'partner' as a basic level worker to narrow the gap of bureaucracy. Furthermore, they co-work in the first line to eliminate the distance between different statuses. Secondly, the numbers of employees are usually from three to six. Such a small size of a retail shop makes staffs acquaint with each other easily and deeply. In the co-working period, this helps a team to match different personalities and majors quickly to achieve well performance. Next, the suggestions and complaints provided by employees are treated of equal importance. In the same way, they have a right to participate in the process of revising company policies as well as a manager. In that case, each staff thinks that they also play an important role in company operations, and they can join to work out a direction for Starbucks. These give employees not only a respect, but a sense of participation.

A Goal of Public Welfare

Starbucks has endeavoured to create a 'third place' (outside from home or office) for people to take a rest (resource: Wikipedia). They want to provide such a comfortable environment to increase the harmoniousness of the society. Apart from this, Starbucks contributes part of its profits to public service; on the other hand, it also set a goal to improve and donate to the society. As a consequence, the aim makes all staff have an idea that what they do for Starbucks is for the society as well. As the goal theory, Starbucks set a challenging and specific goal, and it permits all partners to decide the direction. Afterwards, employees embrace to do what they chose and they get some feedbacks from the goal. The concept causes an increase of the power of agglomerate and enthusiasm in relation with a positive effect to the profit of Starbucks.

Conclusions

Starbucks changes the behaviours and viewpoints of global consumers to coffee, and this successful example has caught global attention. Nevertheless, it was also a small retail coffee shop in North America initially. Nowadays, it is not only one of the fastest-growing corporation, but also an outstanding business model with lower employee turnover rate and higher profit performance. According to the case of Starbucks, it shows that motivation is the key factor of a company policy; in other words, opposite to the principles of classical management which only concerns about producing but ignoring workers' ideas. In recent successful businesses, the appropriate management for labours should include financial and emotional rewards. Besides, motivation and personal satisfaction should be put at first rank. A good relationship between managers and employees could maintain a high quality of performance. Just like Starbucks, to use the correct strategy would lead to a successful path.

Case Questions

1. What are the various methods of motivation and personal satisfaction adopted by Starbucks to enhance the performance of their staff? Which of these are unique?

2. How does Starbucks maintain and ensure healthy relationships amongst its employees?

3. What are the various staff welfare policies adopted by Starbucks?

4. What do you think are the real problems bothering Starbucks? Would these issues have any long-term resolutions in terms of ensuring cultural and strategic fits?

5. In spite of its intense promotional efforts Starbucks has not captured the market share in India in comparison with the ever-popular Nestle Brand and others. What could be the aspects of marketing and pricing strategy which Starbuck needs to adopt?

6. How do you think Café Coffee day is performing in respect of the Beverages market complexity?

7. What are the key learnings for Indian companies derived from the Starbucks example?

5

Great Thought—Difficult for Business

A Case Study in Sustainability Management

Learning Objectives

It has been always a catch 22 situation for majority of projects in Sustainability Management irrespective of considerations on economic, environmental, societal sustainability issues. There has always been strong resistance to all such projects within and between the essential aspects of Sustainability Management. It has mostly been a difficult trade-off between growth and sustainability priorities in conflict with each other.

Synopsis

People watch the actions of leaders, and it resonates, says Mr Albanese, the soft-spoken former top gun at the $47.7 billion mining giant Rio Tinto, who completes one year as CEO of Vedanta group an Indian conglomerate in mining sector. In the implementation and measurement of corporate sustainability the 'Tone from the Top' is critical, especially while attempting to usher in a fundamental change in the corporate culture of a company, which is perhaps the most reviled in global attempts to manage for sustainability.

Over the years, Vedanta has been mauled by civil society campaigns over its human rights record, in India and elsewhere, and has also incurred the wrath of large global investors. According to Albanese, who has issued notes to key levels of management that his two 'no-compromise positions are safety and integrity' even as he looks deeper

Indian Business Case Studies. V P Pawar, Bhagyashree Kunte, and Srinivas Tumuluri, Oxford University Press.
© ASM Group of Institutes, Pune, India 2022. DOI: 10.1093/oso/9780192869388.003.0005

in to the tenets of responsible mining and sustainable development at Vedanta Group.

Senior management at Vedanta also recognizes that Vedanta's social license to operate has been frayed and that it is about time to retrieve the situation. 'We have been unable to operate at our full capacities,' says Albanese, underlining the need to regain trust and the societal license. There is indeed a strong business case to be responsible.

Corporate Social Responsibility (CSR) measures are certainly welcome, but it can only be a small component of an overall approach. While Albanese is deeply appreciative of Vedanta's CSR programmes, he is clearly uncomfortable with the charity of approach; the idea of creating a 'dependency relationship' between a company and communities.

Arvind Khare of the US-based rights and resources initiative speaks in the same vein and explains that the Indian Land Acquisition Bill will do little to ameliorate conflicts in India as long as the legitimate claims of communities on forests, wastelands, commons, or pastures are not recognized.

Today Vedanta needs a very refined approach to sustainable mining. The company should mandate 'cultural heritage assessments', of mining sites. It even should seek 'disturbance approval' from communities, with a non-compromising objective that indigenous peoples ought to be the 'drivers of their own destinies' and that they have 'a share in the wealth generated by mining activities'.

The Vedanta story would have been quite different if it had a degree of sensitivity to the cultural traditions of the Dongria-Kondhs who venerate the Niyamgiri hills in India as their god.

What Vedanta Claims

Our Approach

Our vision is to be a leading, diversified natural resources company providing superior returns to our shareholders—a journey we have been on for a decade. We will meet our vision by delivering high-quality assets and low-cost operations, with sustainable development at the core of all that we do.

Our Strategy

We aim to deliver growth and long-term value while upholding sustainable development through our diversified portfolio of large, long-life, and low-cost assets. Our sustainability model, which comprises the three pillars of responsible stewardship, building strong relationships, and adding and sharing value, provides us with a robust structure for driving our future growth, advancing our business outcomes, and offering significant benefits to the communities that host our operations.

Our Sustainability Model

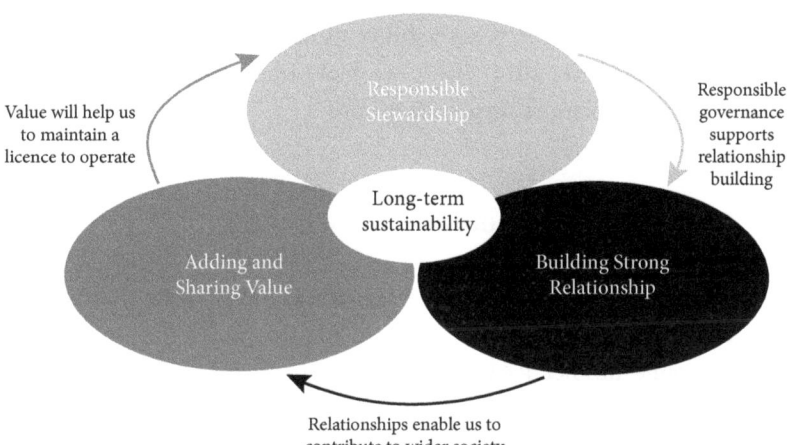

Responsible stewardship means ensuring we have effective and appropriate business processes, including robust compliance and risk management, protecting the health and safety of our employees, and responsibly managing our environmental and social impacts.

Building strong relationships captures our engagement with the people and organizations that are interested in our business. Doing this effectively can lead to the identification of new areas where we can find and unlock additional value as well as equipping us to foresee and appropriately manage challenges.

Adding and sharing value encapsulates the direct and indirect positive economic impact we make, by investing in people through employment;

building infrastructure; developing technology; and the payment of taxes, royalties, and other payments to local, state, and national governments. Additionally, it captures the value we offer by turning the knowledge and ideas sourced through engagement with our stakeholders into specific projects, including collaborating with governments and NGOs to bring value to the communities that host our operations.

Our three pillars guide our stakeholder engagement and help us to build trusted relationships. As a consequence of these engagements and to respond to stakeholders' areas of interest we developed our sustainability framework. The framework comprises policies, technical standards, management standards, and guidance notes across the three pillars to establish clear standards, set targets for improving performance, and maximize value to our stakeholders.

Since introducing our sustainability model and supporting sustainability framework in 2011–2012, we have implemented our policies, standards, and processes across the group.

Community at the Centre

Albanese the new CEO of Vedanta says it was unfortunate that Vedanta allowed the Niyamgiri issue to fester and turn 'iconic'. Communities, with greater mobile and net access, are more aware of and are standing up for their rights. International institutions are pitching in with binding and voluntary norms: the ILO Convention 169, the UN Declaration on the Rights of Indigenous Peoples, the UN Principles on Human Rights and Businesses, and, more recently, the revised IFC performance standards.

Albanese is therefore endeavouring to align the company to emerging global trends in responsibility—be it human rights, biodiversity protection, or the growing traction on Free Prior and Informed Consent (FPIC)—while dealing with land and communities. He is also taking Vedanta into the International Council on Mining and Metals (ICMM), which is focused on the sustainability performance of extractive companies. The ICMM as a standards-setting outfit has catalysed improvements in the extractive sector. Last year, for instance, around 15% of its membership vowed to consider the 'no-go' option, even for prospecting, in areas of high biodiversity value.

Can Vedanta, considering where it is today, absorb and measure up to global sustainability standards? Albanese is certain it can, for it has performed reasonably well in certain aspects of sustainability. 'If a company is weak in any individual part of sustainability, everything falls apart,' he says. He is also aware that it will take time for the transformation to happen; that is the reason why he is pacing the process and working on multiple fronts. On taking over as CEO he didn't try a bring-down-and-rebuild approach. 'Bending and molding is my way,' he says.

Also demonstrating sustainability leadership immediately on taking over he made it clear that safety and integrity would be the cornerstone of his drive. Employees are perplexed when he frowns on people who don't use the support rails while climbing or coming down flights of stairs.

A Fresh Perspective

Safety is a huge challenge for the group. The chimney collapse, which saw the death of 45 people at the Balco plant in Korba in 2009, still rankles. Vedanta recorded 19 fatal accidents in 2013–2014. It's down to five this year; eight including the Konkola Copper Mines in Zambia (while Rio Tinto with operations in 40 countries had only three fatalities in the same period). Albanese wants to move to a zero-fatalities scenario.

While internally there is a new engagement with employees, both chairman Agarwal and Albanese are sending signals about the shift in attitudes to outside stakeholders too. The duo has made it clear that the company will not mine in areas 'without the express invitation and free prior agreement of the local communities to do so'. While a court process has already seen the Niyamgiri palli sabhas say 'no' to bauxite mining, the unambiguous proclamation and stand on 'consent' is an attempt to 'create a cleaner picture around brand Vedanta'.

It's still work in progress. The stranglehold of people from accounting, finance, and engineering on company matters is, or was, complete and absolute in Vedanta. This had to be broken to engender some sensitivity towards sustainable development. One may acquire the cognitive skills but may not get the lateral bandwidth; the full intuitive understanding of a resources company. Expanding this bandwidth to embrace views not just from these narrow confines can lead to change. Explains Albanese—We now look at issues from a fresh set of eyes and what precisely are the sustainability issues most relevant to the company? To get a hold on this, a materiality mapping was done. As expected safety, waste, water, emissions, community management, approach to new projects were high priority. The surprise element in the matrix was the need to address biodiversity issues. For most Indian companies, biodiversity does not figure on the agenda but it's gaining traction globally.

For mining companies, biodiversity conservation is integral to securing the social license to operate. (Rio Tinto pursues a policy of Net Positive Impact (NPI), which refers to a point where biodiversity gains exceed biodiversity loss due to mining or other project activities.)

Albanese concedes that NPI is extremely difficult and can only be rational for many as he recalls the complex modelling and biodiversity offset principles he had to wade through in his previous job. For Vedanta, he prescribes a policy of 'No Net Loss' (NNL) in the mitigation hierarchy (NNL ensures there is no overall reduction in the type, amount, and condition of biodiversity over space and time).

Albanese is also passionate about transparency and would like to soon emulate an industry first from his previous company; reporting on the economic contributions made by a company to public finances; all listed out in the most granular fashion. A quick scan of the company's 20-page tax paid report of 2014 reveals that Rio Tinto, with a very marginal presence in India (the Bunder project), paid $4 million in taxes to the Indian government and $1 million to Madhya Pradesh, 'a "tax paid report" is a valuable document; it allows you to engage with stakeholders on this vital issue,' says Albanese.

For Vedanta, which has faced tax demands in Zambia, and continues to face them in India, some sunshine on taxes paid is welcome. The sustainability agenda is clearly kicking in it looks like?

With global sustainability regulations getting very stringent how would Vedanta be able to take a leadership role in its sustainability management efforts is yet to be seen. The political will and the regulatory controls as resisted by the clouded understanding of simultaneous management of sustainability and growth are the real challenges for mining industries in India. While issues such as a forestation and dislocation of adivasis from their naturalized habitats are being partly real and partly created and fully exploited by the middlemen it looks like a real uphill task for India to raise to the call of global community towards ensuring sustainability on the planet Earth.

Even the CSR norms as revised in the recent amendments to the companies act and the listing agreements are being contested for clarity and attempts to find loopholes in the law are rampant as ever. There is already a great hue and cry about the amendments to the land acquisition bill in the governmental levels and it's easy for the land mafias to exploit the situation to the detriment of the common man and his sustainable future. Projects with high promise of economic growth literally each one of them need to be vetted by sustainability clause unless there is clarity of understanding of objectives and impacts of sustainability measures from a very long-term points of view devoid of greed and small mind approach to prosperity through improved quality of life. Individual entities like Vedanta will continue to face the proverbial catch 22 situation blamed for non-compliance and equally guilty of following the socio-political hidden agenda.

Some Food for Thoughts on Sustainable Management

Costs of the Conflict

The study, conducted by the Harvard Kennedy School and the Centre for Social Responsibility in Mining, Australia, indicate a world-class mining project (capital expenditure between $3 billion and $5 billion) stands to lose approximately $20 million per week of delayed production in Net Present Value (NPV) due to lost sales arising out of conflicts.

It was also revealed that fire-fighting after things have gone terribly wrong in the project life cycle is not the right approach as the relationship with the community, even if mended, can be fragile. Engagement and measures to prevent conflict have to happen before the start of the project.

Another recent study by the Washington DC-based rights and resources initiative reveals land issues that lead to social conflict can increase operating costs of companies by as much as 29 times over a baseline scenario. The situation is indeed grim as future global reserves are largely spread over indigenous peoples' or tribal lands; 50% for oil and gas production and 80% for mining. In India, a quarter of the districts are already affected. Conflicts will only increase, says Arvind Khare, executive director, Rights and Resources Group of the Initiative.

Free Prior and Informed Consent

While the present government attempts to water down consent requirements in the Land Acquisition Bill and other laws, the world, including large mining and oil and gas corporations, is headed in the opposite direction.

The concept of FPIC, while dealing with tribal or indigenous communities is gaining traction in national law, international norms, and voluntary best practice standards. Land rights therefore have moved beyond the realms of narrow social justice debates. It's now all about democratic rights, equity-driven economic development, and environmental sustainability. FPIC, as the term suggests, is much more nuanced than consultation or plain-vanilla consent. Iterations are still being debated but it is generally agreed that FPIC also lends indigenous communities the right to say 'no' to a project or even refrain from engaging on the issue. The financial sector is also cleaning up its act. The IFC of the World Bank Group, in its revised performance standards, embraces FPIC.

This automatically brings in over 80 financial institutions in 35 countries that have signed up for the 'Equator Principles' into the fold. The Equator banks cover 70% of international project finance debt in emerging markets. The FPIC guidelines of the International Council for Mining and Metals, with almost all major global mining corporations as members, come into effect from May 2015. The sticky part, however, emerges when national standards are lower than FPIC as is the situation in India. How do multinationals navigate this issue? Tom Albanese, Vedanta CEO, is guarded, and maintains mining companies cannot override national legislation or impinge on the sovereign rights of a country.

The international community has addressed this issue. For instance, the UN special rapporteur on indigenous peoples' rights has clarified that companies must respect the rights of indigenous peoples even 'in cases where states are opposed to the application of making FPIC a reality'.

Coexistence and Benefit-Sharing

For over 40 years, the aboriginal communities of Weipa in Australia were in constant skirmish with the mining company Comalco (now Rio Tinto Alcan). The region constitutes one of the world's largest bauxite reserves covering 3,860 sq. km. A truce emerged only in 2001 with the signing of the Western Cape Communities Co-existence Agreement (WCCCA) between the company, the communities of the region, local councils, and the Queensland government.

It took them five years of hard negotiations. At the signing ceremony, the acting CEO of the company Keith Johnson promised a fresh beginning and apologized to the communities for taking four decades to realize they could co-exist and prosper together.

The WCCCA goes beyond recognizing land, jobs, and rehabilitation rights; it also includes cultural heritage and environmental protection, land relinquishment plans, and outlines governance structures. Most importantly, it also spells out an extensive benefit sharing programme with the company contributing a minimum of $2.5 million a year and more depending on bauxite production and the market price of aluminium.

Another $ 500,000 a year is spent on capacity building of communities, education, skills training, and now even entrepreneurship development and supplier diversity initiatives. The Queensland government contributes another $1.5 million a year. Around $6 million is invested into the Weipa communities each year. The monies come into a communities trust and 60% of the funds are immediately locked up in long-term secure investments so that future generations also benefit. The mines are expected to be productive for another 40 years. The remaining 40% of the funds are distributed to three sub-regional trusts, which oversee community projects of different aboriginal groups. The entire system is designed to involve direct participation of the communities in the decision-making processes. This is not all. The bouquet of Weipa agreements includes the Weipa Township Agreement: Rio Tinto Alcan is responsible for administering the Weipa town. Obviously, there have been challenges in Weipa but through the years course corrections have happened as businesses and governments now realize that social investments are more than risk mitigation measures.

Case Questions

1. How should one look in to sustainability issues in emerging markets? There appears to be a greater dimension than globalization to the localized issues of poverty, security, and safety in the garb of corruption, exploitation, and fundamentalistic approaches overriding the calls of the planet for pollution control and sustainable business practices.

2. Most of us are aware of the violent demonstrations which took place recently at Vedanta's Sterlite Project in Tamil Nadu after running successfully for 20 years. Sterlite unit has been closed. Similarly the major oil refinery project in Maharashtra (Konkan Area) is being opposed tooth and nail by locals as also by prominent political parties. Same applies to Samruddha Expressway and the Bullet Train Project. How can growth be achieved without infra projects?

3. How should India handle the dilemma of growth vs sustainability development?

SECTION II

CASE STUDIES IN FINANCE MANAGEMENT

Financial Accounting, Direct/ Indirect Taxation, Banking and Insurance

6

Turmoil in the Banking Landscape

A Case Study in the Banking/Finance Sector

Learning Objectives

To understand the capital structure pattern of banking sector with reference to the generation platform. To understand public sector banks, performance of banking in India, the financial industry, developments and
policy responses, and reforms in the Indian banking sector. To understand the various banking products such as loans and advances, non-performing assets, and categories of NPA and to know the process of merger
of banks, recovery tribunal, and role of Reserve Bank of India.

Synopsis

The Indian banking system was initially thought to be insulated from
the global financial crisis owing to heavy public ownership and cautious
management. It was thus a surprise when some banks experienced deposit flight, as depositors shifted their money to government-owned
banks and specifically towards the State Bank of India, the largest
public bank. While there was some tendency for depositors to favour
healthier banks and banks with more stable funding, the reallocation of
deposits towards the State Bank of India cannot be explained by these
factors alone. Rather it appears that the implicit government guarantee

Indian Business Case Studies. V P Pawar, Bhagyashree Kunte, and Srinivas Tumuluri, Oxford University Press.
© ASM Group of Institutes, Pune, India 2022. DOI: 10.1093/oso/9780192869388.003.0006

of the liabilities of the country's largest public bank dominated other considerations.

Introduction

For more than two decades' public sector banks managed to stave off competition due mainly to the trust people had in them due to government backing. As the next generation comes in with different attitude, are they equipped to serve them? They need to reinvent to survive. For half a century since bank nationalization, public sector banks dominated the credit flow to the economy with more than four-fifths of the share. In 2019, the golden jubilee year, private lenders accounted for Rs 69 of every Rs 100 loan. The tables are turning. As the economy adjusts to the new reality like technology-driven financial services, a robust bankruptcy law, vanishing 'phone banking' and plethora of competition from unknown quarters, the Goliaths of Indian finance face the formidable task of remaining relevant—and surviving momentous change.

It's not just the availability of capital that provides strength to give out loans, but the skills and attitude to face the digital world, where customer convenience trumps everything else that would determine their survival. It would not be just deposits that flow because of the comfort of government backing, but also efficient lending that holds the key to their relevance. The collapse of lending, lack of vision, and risk aversion combines to present a muddy picture of state-run banks akin to other state-backed businesses, such as BSNL, Air India, and BHEL, which failed to keep pace with advancements only to turn a pale shadow of their pasts. 'Unless government-owned banks put their house in order, they would see a much faster decline in the coming years and it is difficult to predict whether they will be able to face the onslaught of competition from new-age banks'.

Data shows that government-owned banks' share of total credit outstanding fell to 60% at the end of March 2019 from 75% in 2012. State-run banks disbursed Rs 59.2 lakh crore at the end of March 2019, up 4% or Rs 57 lakh crore, from a year earlier, shows RBI data. By contrast, private-sector peers loaned Rs 33.2 lakh crore in 2019, up nearly a fifth from Rs 26.6 lakh crore a year ago.

Changing Scenario

Public sector banks remained the first port of call for anyone who sought banking services as they evoked trust and faith among people. The state-owned majority stakes in these banks led to the belief that every penny in those banks is safe.

Furthermore, private sector banking services gained notoriety where hidden charges were slicing away customers' funds without them even realizing. There was a belief that state-run banks did not indulge in such. But as the younger generation gets prominence and technology helps improve services, the millennial customer doesn't bother about whether a bank is state-owned or private.

'Public sector banks have to realize there is a new generation of consumers that expect a certain standard of service that perhaps these competitors are providing—be it in terms of the digital experience or technology or branch banking services,' said K Cherian Varghese, former MD, Union Bank of India. That even the seniors are moving into the digital age reflects the surge in electronic payments. Of the total small-ticket retail transactions worth Rs 10.32 lakh crore in March 2019, the share of online deals has risen to 61%, up almost three times from 24% in March 2016. In the payment space, digital wallets and non-bank Unified Payments Interface (UPI) players had a share of 14.7% in March 2019, up from 1.6% in the same period in 2016. Also, the key function of payments is being facilitated by the likes of Paytm and PhonePe reducing the reliance on bank platforms.

Talent to Compete

The biggest differentiator has been the lack of specialized manpower at state-owned banks. The government recently announced its intent to fill middle-management positions at state-run banks and offer them a longer tenure. Nearly 70% of mid-management staff at PSU banks is over 50 years of age, suggesting their retirement isn't too far away.

'While the PSBs have the entire necessary infrastructure in place such as the core banking systems and Internet banking solutions, it is the workforce that needs to be reoriented and retrained,' said Varghese. 'The attitude needs to change; there is a need for a ground level training exercise conducted by the government to bring the PSB staff and bankers in tune with the market best practices.' State-owned banks are also constrained due to compensation they offer and senior PSU executives time and again have demanded they be allowed to hire a portion of their recruits the way private sector banks do, so that the best talent pools are also available to them.

'PSU banks need to change their people strategy, put more feet on the street, redeploy its current manpower, train them for specialized functions, initiate lateral hires for specific functions and every bank depending upon their strength needs to bring in a board-approved, market linked compensation,' said Sur.

Legacy Drag

State-run banks, because of their ownership structure, were functioning more like a ward of the government rather than like businesses that are supposed to make profits. These lenders became tools for the governments to carry out their welfare agenda.

Also, cronyism led to many decisions being influenced and led to unviable projects getting funded. The last two decades saw an enormous surge in funding private infrastructure projects that led to a huge pile-up of bad loans. Data showed that PSU banks had a gross NPA ratio of 11.6% at the end of March 2019 and contributed nearly Rs 7.39 lakh crore to the total bad loan pile of Rs 9.36 lakh crore. Private Banks on the other hand had a GNPA ratio of 5.3% with Rs 1.83 lakh crore as bad loans in value terms. As state-run lenders got hobbled by bad loans, private banks stepped on the gas to secure more deposits. State-owned banks' total deposit base was at Rs 84.86 lakh crore at the end of March 2019, up from Rs 82.62 lakh crore a year ago. Private Banks' deposits rose 25% to Rs 37.7 lakh crore. But public sector banks believe that weakening metrics are just temporary and that they could roar back. Meanwhile, private lenders are turning more efficient than their state-owned peers. The spreads for PSU banks were at 2.8% for 2019 and 2.5% for 2018, while private banks had a spread of 3.6% in both 2019 and 2018, RBI data showed. Their cost of funds and cost of deposits were almost identical.

Baby Steps

PSU banks are also facing fierce competition not only from private peers but also from small finance banks, fin techs, non-bank lenders, and micro-finance institutions. And the competition is only getting fierce. Small finance banks showed impressive growth with their total loans growing to Rs 59,491 crore versus Rs 34,879 crore, a growth of more than 70% in a year.

Banks which own the customers and have their deposits saw their control in the overall transactional pie gradually reducing to 81% from 92.7% three years ago. As PSU banks realize that they could not do it on their own, they are looking to partner with these nimble firms in their catch-up act.

'Well, obviously we see competition from a host of entities that are trying to get a piece of PSUs' original home turf, especially in rural and semi urban areas,' says Mahapatra of Syndicate Bank. 'Going forward, we see use of technology and collaboration as small finance banks, MFIs, non-banks are good at this, and we see huge opportunities in co origination.' But these banks also face sudden distractions. Last year was significant in the sense that the government moved to consolidate many banks that would make them bigger, but not necessarily more efficient and competitive. The government decided to merge 10 state-run banks into four, including Oriental Bank of Commerce and United Bank of India with Punjab National Bank; Andhra Bank and Corporation Bank with Union Bank of India, opening up a new opportunity.

'Merger has given them a chance to redefine them,' says PwC's Sur. 'Today, all of them are copycats of each other; better and bigger banks will bring in more capital, talented workforce and the power of the combined entity.'

'While the process could slow them down as not all of them are on the same technology platform, there's hope of revival. With mergers playing out in 2020, the professionalization of state-run banks will accelerate for the rank and file, it will be business as usual; it will be time consuming for the top management. But you will see state run banks bearing the benefits of this merger in the times to come', says one of the CEOs of a public sector bank.

This year would also see two private sector banks, ICICI Bank and Axis Bank, which were dragged down by bad loans, make up for the lost time. Mergers and government's investment of nearly Rs 3 lakh crore as capital in the past few years have ensured that they don't sink. But the field has gotten a lot more competitive that would force state-run banks to come up with new ways to survive.

'India is in the classic Darwinian mode of what I call survival of the fittest,' said Uday Kotak, founder of Kotak Mahindra. Reserve Bank of India (RBI) has decided to set up Public Credit Registry (PCR) an extensive database of credit information which is accessible to all stakeholders. The Insolvency and Bankruptcy Code (Amendment) Ordinance, 2017 Bill has been passed and is expected to strengthen the banking sector. In June 2019, RBI sets average base rate of 9.18% for non-banking financial companies and microfinance institutions borrowers for the quarter beginning of July.

Deposits under Pradhan Mantri Jan Dhan Yojana (PMJDY) increased to Rs 98,320 crore (US$ 14.07 billion) and 355.4 million accounts were opened in India (as of 29 May 2019). In May 2018, the Government of India provided Rs 6 lakh crore (US$ 93.1 billion) loans to 120 million beneficiaries under Mudra scheme. Under PMJDY, more than Rs 1 lakh crore (US$ 14.30 billion) have been deposited till July 2019. In May 2018, the total number of subscribers was 11 million, under Atal Pension Yojna.

Rising incomes are expected to enhance the need for banking services in rural areas and therefore drive the growth of the sector. As of September 2018, Department of Financial Services (DFS), Ministry of Finance, and National Informatics Centre (NIC) launched Jan Dhan Darshak as a part of financial inclusion initiative. It is a mobile app to help people locate financial services in India.

The digital payments revolution will trigger massive changes in the way credit is disbursed in India. Debit cards have radically replaced credit cards as the preferred payment mode in India, after demonetization. Transactions through UPI stood at 955 million in September 2019 worth Rs 161,457 crore (US$ 23.10 billion).

As per Union Budget 2019–2020, the government has proposed a fully automated GST refund module and an electronic invoice system that will eliminate the need for a separate e-way bill.

Future Imperfect

As per the above discussion, we can say that the biggest challenge for banking industry is to serve the mass market of India. Companies have shifted their focus from product to customer. The better we understand our customers, the more successful we will be in meeting their needs. In order to mitigate above-mentioned challenges Indian banks must cut their cost of their services. Another aspect to encounter the challenges is product differentiation. Apart from traditional banking services, Indian banks must adopt some product innovation so that they can compete in gamut of competition. Technology up-gradation is an inevitable aspect to face challenges. The level of consumer awareness is significantly higher as compared to previous years. Now-a-days they need internet banking, mobile banking and ATM services. Expansion of branch size in order to increase market share is another tool to combat competitors. Therefore, Indian nationalized and private sector banks must spread their wings towards global markets as some of them have already done it. Indian banks are trustworthy brands in Indian market; therefore, these banks must utilize their brand equity as it is a valuable asset for them.

Conclusions

Over the years, it has been observed that clouds of trepidation and drops of growth are two important phenomena of market, which frequently changes in different sets of conditions. The pre- and post-liberalization era has witnessed various environmental changes which directly affects the aforesaid phenomenon. It is evident that post-liberalization era has spread new colours of growth in India, but simultaneously it has also posed some challenges.

This case discusses the various challenges and opportunities like rural market, transparency, customer expectations, management of risks, growth in banking sector, human factor, global banking, environmental concern, social, ethical issues, employee and customer retentions. Banks are striving to combat the competition. The competition from global banks and technological innovation has compelled the banks to rethink their policies and strategies.

Case Questions

1. Discuss the recent developments of Indian Banking Sector.

2. Is there a need of Financial Inclusion in the banking industry?

3. What are the steps to be taken by Reserve Bank of India to maintain the liquidity in the banking institution?

7

Information Technology and Banking Industry

A Case Study in IT and Banking

Learning Objectives

To study strategies built and executed by organizations to manage change. To learn the reasons behind/which brings change in economy. To study the emergence of ICT and e-business sector in globalized age. To understand the flow charts used by ICT to ensure coordination, communication in the organization. To study the role of e-business sector in asking the organization to meet manage coordination leadership and clear communication. To understand and study techniques of ICT for smooth functioning of organization.

Synopsis

Banking corporations in the public sector always seem to be change resistant in the banking sector. Being one of them as a result many private and public sector banking corporations are opting to go for capacity and not change. Hence, it becomes important to ensure good coordination, strong leadership, and clear communication while managing various changes simultaneously. There are three major trends those shape change. Specifically, the three trends are the intensified competition brought through globalization, information technology, and managerial innovation. Globalization is changing the economy and markets in which organizations operate. And there has been an increase in the e-business

Indian Business Case Studies. V P Pawar, Bhagyashree Kunte, and Srinivas Tumuluri, Oxford University Press.
© ASM Group of Institutes, Pune, India 2022. DOI: 10.1093/oso/9780192869388.003.0007

sector that is changing the method of distribution of work and its performance with the use of information and communication technology (ICT).
Moreover, managerial innovation becomes more important as a form of
response to both competition and information technology trends.

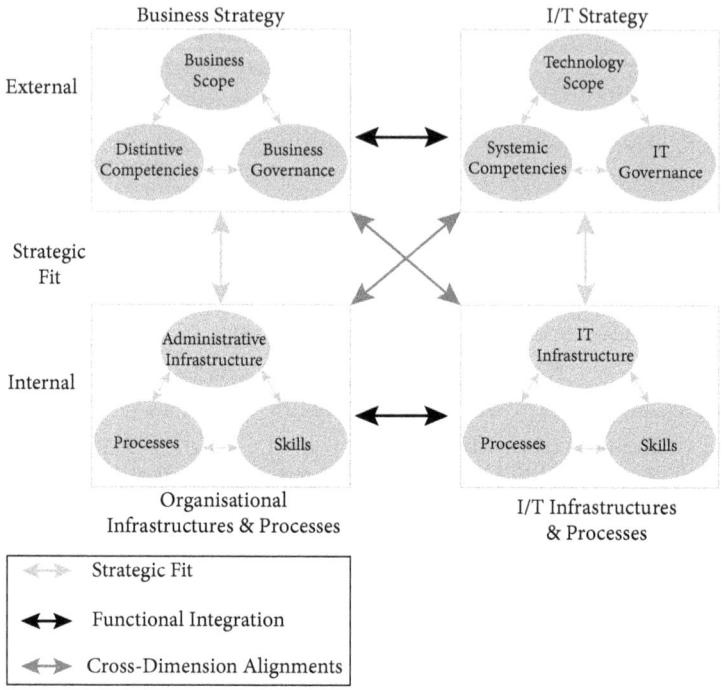

Figure 7.1 Functional Integration

Figure 7.1 shows the model alignment of the four domains (external
and internal domains). Also, the figure further explains the views of external domains connected to strategic fit and internal domains across all
business and IT sectors. To decide the organization infrastructure, strategic action can also be applied while information technology is directly
related to functional integration and alignment of the organization. The
linking together of components, quadrants as a unit, functional integration, and strategic fit is very important in an organization. According to
James Brown and Elizabeth Arriazza, for the strategy to be accomplished,
IS infrastructure and the design selection of the organization is seen as
the basis to be properly articulated with the business plan. The strategy

execution way of doing things has now improved the change in organization infrastructure.

Use of Information Assets in Strategic Decision Making

The data gathered in an organization keeps increasing day by day. Thus most organizations will consider collection of clients data as a vital information and probably the most relevant strategic asset held. The information asset gathered must be exploited properly and guided jealously. Examples of information asset are listed below in Figure 7.2:

- ✓ Financial Record
- ✓ Database of contacts
- ✓ Records compared with a particular project

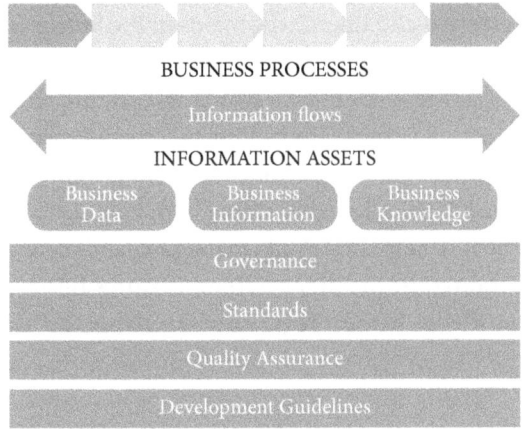

Figure 7.2 Information Asset for Strategic Decision Making
(*Source*: eacademy, 2015)

The Future Imperfect

Emergence of the e-business is due to globalization and the ICT gives a fine and advanced model to have interlinks among departments and link the business units with external world. It eases and confirms accurate management of work from top level to bottom level. The strategies defined by firms using ICT model helps proper execution of work, best management functions, and appropriate communication network at internal and external domains. Organizers should check upon cash flows, financial budget continuously in order to adapt new technology and overcome its cost brilliantly to change infrastructure and provide required resources and train the staff to produce accordingly and survive strongly in the global business environment. Youth Chinese Test (YCT) provides good decisions, best standards assured quality, and development guidelines.

Conclusions

Organizations need to use ICT to manage change raised through globalization which has emerged as the e-business sector. A strong coordination between external and internal domains of the business organization is necessary. It requires strong management and business strategies to be adopted and for it, there has to be a strong integration among corporate business and functional units. The linking together of components, quadrants as a unit, functional integration, and strategic fit is very important in an organization It helps in maintaining high volumes of data of the organizations. The ICT helps in storing, managing, and communicating the information required in the organization. It stores business data information and knowledge to meet regulatory standards and assures quality.

Case Questions

1. Analyse the case in terms of the latest systems adopted.

2. What are the essentials for an organization to follow the strategies to manage change?

3. How is e-business sector leading over other business sectors?

8

ING Vysya Bank vs Kotak Mahindra Bank

A Case Study on Bank Mergers

Learning Objectives

Bank mergers have been a major part of financial restructuring activity and also included as an important part of annual national budget exercise in India of late. In fact the current year's budget is more focused on privatizing of public sector banks as completely in opposition of the bank nationalization programme implemented in the early 1970s and 1980s. The present case study about two major banks in the private sector venturing to merge basically to en-cash on the operating synergies as also rebuilding customer confidence when one of the banks involved has a tendency to performance failures and management issues. This case study therefore brings up the real objectives of both strategic growth strategy and also issue of survival and revival of an ailing bank.

Synopsis

The case study is about the merger deal between ING Vysya Bank and Kotak Mahindra Bank. The deal created the fourth largest private sector bank in the Indian banking industry. The case provides enough material to discuss the dynamics and the mergers in the Indian banking industry. The case also provides enough material to analyse and discuss the synergies and challenges of the merger deal of ING Vysya and Kotak Mahindra bank.

Indian Business Case Studies. V P Pawar, Bhagyashree Kunte, and Srinivas Tumuluri, Oxford University Press.
© ASM Group of Institutes, Pune, India 2022. DOI: 10.1093/oso/9780192869388.003.0008

Case Details

In November 2014, Kotak Mahindra Bank Limited (Kotak) announced its acquisition of ING Vysya Bank Limited (ING Vysya), a quasi-foreign bank owned by Dutch multinational, the ING Group in a full-share deal worth of US$2.4 billion. The deal, the biggest in the Indian banking sector, created the fourth largest private bank in India with a balance sheet size of Rs 2 trillion and market capitalization of over Rs 1 trillion. According to industry experts, this deal helped Kotak to expand its presence in India and to compete with other top-notch private sector players in the Indian banking industry. The amalgamation is subject to the approval of the shareholders of Kotak and ING Vysya respectively, Reserve Bank of India under the Banking Regulation Act, the Competition Commission of India and such other regulatory approvals as may be required. Upon obtaining all approvals, when the merger becomes effective, ING Vysya will merge with Kotak. Shareholders of ING Vysya will receive shares of Kotak in exchange of shares in ING Vysya at the approved share exchange ('swap') ratio. All shareholders of Kotak and ING Vysya will participate thereafter in the (merged) Kotak business. All ING Vysya branches and employees will become Kotak branches and employees. ING Vysya's CEO designate, Mr Uday Sareen, will be inducted into the top management of Kotak reporting directly to Mr Uday Kotak, executive vice chairman and managing director of Kotak.

According to experts, the Indian banking sector needed such mergers not only to create world-sized banks to compete with foreign banks but also to create banks with a sufficient capital base to fund various large infrastructure projects crucial to maintain the growth of India economy.

However, industry experts had doubts on the synergies of the merger. They quoted a study by KPMG and Wharton which found 83% of Merger and Acquisitions (M&A) failed to produce any benefits and over half of M&A ended up reducing shareholder value instead of increasing it. Some experts were worried about the various challenges the merger deal threw up, such as the cultural differences between the two banks and the reaction of the employees union among others. However, other experts were positive about the deal.

Indian Banking Industry

Since ancient times, an indigenous banking industry had prevailed in India with some communities being traditionally involved. These communities mostly ran huge businesses apart from the banking business. In fact, the banking business was relatively smaller than their other businesses. They mainly dealt in money lending, did not accept deposits from customers, and discouraged savings.

They used their personal wealth and that of their ancestors and income from other businesses for lending purposes. They lent money for personal as well as business purposes and were infamous for the high rates of interest they charged and their unethical banking practices.

M&A Activity in Indian Banking Sector

The Western type of banks came into the picture in the late 18th century in India when Bank of Hindustan was established in 1770 in Calcutta (now Kolkata) in Western India. Later, General Bank of India was established in 1786 in Calcutta. Calcutta became the centre of banking activities mainly due to the trading activities of British Empire. In the 19th century, the major development in the Indian banking industry was the establishment of three presidency banks by the British East India Company. However, in 1921, these three presidency banks were amalgamated to create the Imperial Bank of India.

The Indian banking sector did not witness too many M&A activities when compared to Western and other countries. After the first stage of nationalization in 1969, only 34 mergers took place in the Indian banking sector. In 26 of these deals, PSBs acquired private sector banks that were on the brink of failure, mostly on a directive from the RBI. The remaining eight deals happened between private sector banks.

The merger prior to the Kotak and ING Vysya merger in the private sector banking space took place in 2010 when Bank of Rajasthan merged with ICICI Bank in a US$398 million deal. There were many reasons for the low number of M&As in India. These included restrictive regulations, a major part of the banking industry being owned by the Indian government, and the rigid resistance by strong employees unions.

About Kotak

Kotak started as a Non-Banking Financial Company (NBFC)—Kotak Mahindra Capital Management Finance Limited (KMCMFL)—in 1985 in India. KMCMFL was renamed Kotak Mahindra Finance Limited (KMFL) in 1985 and it received its banking license in February 2003 to become the first NBFC to be converted into a full-fledged private bank in India. It was renamed as Kotak Mahindra Bank Limited (Kotak). The consolidated balance sheet of Kotak Mahindra Group is over Rs 1.34 lakh crore and the consolidated net worth of the Group stands at Rs 20,554 crore (approx. US$ 3.3 billion) as on 30 September 2014. The Group offers a wide range of financial services that encompass every sphere of life. From commercial banking to stock broking, mutual funds, life insurance, and investment banking, the Group caters to the diverse financial needs of individuals and the corporate sector. The Group has a wide distribution network through branches and franchisees across India, and international offices in London, New York, Dubai, Abu Dhabi, Mauritius, and Singapore.

Kotak Mahindra Bank

Kotak Mahindra Bank (KMB) offers complete retail financial solutions for varied customer requirements. The Savings Bank Account goes beyond the traditional role of savings, and provides a wide range of services through a comprehensive suite of investment services and other transactional conveniences like online shopping, bill payments, ASBA, Netc@rd, ActivMoney (Automatic TD sweep-in and Sweep-out), etc. Kotak's Jifi, a first-of-its-kind fully integrated Social Bank Account, redefines digital banking by seamlessly incorporating social networking platforms like Twitter and Facebook with mainstream banking. KayPay, the world's first bank agnostic payment product for Facebook users, enables millions of bank account holders transfer money to each other at any hour of the day or night, without the need of net banking, or knowing various bank account related details of the payee. KMBL also offers an investment account where mutual fund investments are recorded and can be viewed in a consolidated fashion across fund houses and schemes. Further, the bank offers loan products such as home loans, personal loans, commercial vehicle loans, etc. Keeping in mind the diverse needs of the business community, KMBL offers comprehensive business solutions that include current accounts, trade services, cash management services, and credit facilities.

About ING

ING Vysya was incorporated as Vysya Bank Limited (Vysya Bank) in 1930 in Bangalore, Karnataka, in Southern India. In 2002, ING Vysya came into existence when the ING Group acquired a major stake in Vysya Bank. This was the first acquisition of an Indian bank by any foreign bank. ING Vysya offered various financial services under four business segments—treasury, corporate/wholesale banking, retail banking, and other banking operations. At the end of FY14, ING Vysya had generated revenue of Rs 60.72 billion with a net profit of Rs 6.58 billion. ING Vysya Bank Ltd is a premier private sector bank with retail, private, and wholesale banking platforms that serve over two million customers. With over 80 years of history in India and leveraging ING's global financial expertise, the bank offers a broad range of innovative and established products and services, across its 573 branches. The bank, which has close to 10,000 employees, is also listed in Bombay Stock Exchange Limited and National Stock Exchange of India Limited. ING Vysya Bank was ranked among the top 5 Most Trusted Brands among private sector banks in India in the Economic Times Brand Equity—Nielsen survey 2011. ING is a global financial institution of Dutch origin offering banking services through its operating company ING Bank and holds significant stakes in listed insurers NN Group NV and Voya Financial, Inc. ING Bank's 53,000 employees offer retail and commercial banking services to customers in over 40 countries.

Merger Deal

On 20 November 2014, Kotak announced the merger with ING Vysya in an all-stock deal worth of Rs 148.51 billion or US$2.4 billion. On regulatory approval, all of ING Vysya's branches and businesses would merge with Kotak. ING Vysya's shareholders would get 0.725 share of Kotak stock for every one stock of ING Vysya they held, i.e., 725 shares of Kotak for every 1,000 shares of ING Vysya. This exchange ratio indicated that the implied price of each stock of ING Vysya was Rs 790 which was based on the average stock price of Kotak and ING Vysya for one month—from 20 October 2014 to 19 November 2014—which came to Rs 1089.50 and Rs 682 respectively.

1) Stock swap: Deals can be conducted in cash or by exchange shares. The Kotak-ING Vysya deal will purely an exchange of stocks. Investors in ING Vysya will get 725 Kotak Mahindra Bank shares for every 1000 ING Vysya shares they held. This means every Kotak share is worth nearly 1.4 shares of ING Vysya. The deal values each share of ING Vysya at Rs 790, much lower than its Thursday closing price of Rs 816.95. However, it is 16% more than the average share price of the ING stock. This means Kotak is paying slightly more than the market price to buy the smaller bank. The entire deal would be valued at over Rs 15,000 crore or $2.4 billion, one of the largest ever.

2) Fourth biggest private bank: The acquisition will create the fourth largest private sector bank in India in terms of branch network. The combined entity will have a market capitalization of Rs 1 lakh crore. This is lower than the market capitalizations of HDFC Bank (Rs 2.2 lakh crore), ICICI Bank (Rs 1.98 lakh crore), and Axis Bank (Rs 1.14 lakh crore)—three of the largest private sector banks in India.

3) Shareholding: Uday Kotak will remain to be the key promoter, holding around 34% stake in the merged bank. This is down from 40%. As per shareholding rules, he has to reduce his stake further to 20% over the next four years. Dutch lender ING Group NV will be the second largest shareholder in the new Kotak Mahindra bank after the deal. It held nearly 43% stake in ING Vysya. Its shareholding in the new entity would be nearly 25.3%, according to an Economic Times report.

4) Brokerages give thumbs up: Most analysts and brokerage firms cheered the deal. This is because they expect the deal to improve Kotak Mahindra's bank business by expanding its branch network

as well as improving its loan portfolio. The deal also happens at a time when the economy is showing signs of improvement. This means, Kotak will be in a better position to take advantage of any rise in demand for loans, analysts said. The deal is likely to increase Kotak's loan book by nearly two-thirds (75%), broker-ages said.

5) Branch network: The merger is expected to double Kotak's branch network from 641 to 1,214 having nearly 40,000 employees. ING Vysya current has about 573 branches in the country, most of which are situated in the South. This is good news is because Kotak was predominantly present in North India. This means the two bank's branches do not overlap. The merger also means the combined en-tity will have a far wider reach in the country than earlier. Kotak is expected to gain 2 million customers from the merger.

6) SME banking: ING Vysya also brings its SME banking platform to the table. This will help Kotak in the long run. As of September, ING Vysya lent about 70% of its total loans to small and medium enterprises (SME) and large companies. In contrast, Kotak lent only 55%. The merger is thus likely to strengthen Kotak's corpo-rate lending business. All of this is expected to increase Kotak's total earnings by one-fifth or 20%, experts suggest.

7) First profitable bank merger since 2008: The banking sector rarely sees a lot of mergers and acquisitions. This is because of strong rules which restrict such movements. Since the 2008 banking crisis, there have been only two deals. However, both the deals involved a profitable bank taking over a smaller loss-making entity. The Kotak Mahindra-ING Vysya deal will be the first since 2008 involving two profit-making banks.

The merger increased the geographical presence and further deepened Kotak's network, thanks to the complementary network of ING Vysya. The merger increased Kotak's number of branches and its ATMs net-work by 47% and 35% to 1,214 and 1,794 respectively. Before the merger, 80% of the Kotak's branches were in the western and northern parts of the country and only 15% were in the southern part of India. On the other hand, ING Vysya had a greater presence in the southern part of the country with 64% of its branches located there and only 32% of its branches in the western and northern parts of the country. After the merger, Kotak had a balanced presence in different parts of the country.

The major challenge was related to human resource management. The salary structure of both banks was also quite different. Around one-third employees of the 10,591 employees of ING Vysya were unionized and their pay structure came under the Indian Banks Association. The employees of ING Vysya were worried whether their pay structure would continue or not. Some of the employees of ING Vysya had other concerns too. Employees in positions like regional manager, sales head, zonal manager, etc., were apprehensive that duplication of positions could lead to transfers or even to their losing their jobs.

According to experts, completing the deal under the nose of the employees' union was the big challenge for Kotak as the employees had already threatened to go on strike on the issue. In 2009, a merger deal between Federal Bank and Catholic Syrian Bank Ltd. did not go through due to the employees union. The troubles for Kotak were compounded when the Securities and Exchange Board of India (SEBI) started an investigation into unusual trading in the shares of Kotak and ING Vysya before the merger was announced in November 2014.

Questions to Discuss

1. Discuss and debate whether the merger deal between Kotak and ING Vysya would help the Indian banking industry.

2. Discuss the synergies of the merger between ING Vysya and Kotak.

3. Understand the challenges faced by the merged Kotak going forward and explore the ways in which it can overcome these challenges.

9

The Ghost of NPAs

A Case Study on Mounting NPAs at PSBs in India

Synopsis

Balance sheets as per norms have to reveal the true positions of the business. Question is do balance sheets of banks do this? Unfortunately they do not. Accounts are shown in assets side but they are not so and are classified as non-performing so what made them to non-perform and what are its effects.

The move on the part of the government to inject capital of Rs 2.11 lakh crore into public sector banks (PSBs) gives strength to the above fact. Why this has to be done and is this enough is the question. In making this move, there was an implied acceptance that the recovery process set up through the Insolvency and Bankruptcy Code (IBC) reform had not been working at the desired pace. When the Reserve Bank of India (RBI) asked PSBs to work on the recovery process for 12 large exposures which account for 50% of the total non-performing assets (NPAs) worth Rs 8 lakh crore in the banking system, it was expected that by December 2017, the banks would recover about Rs 2 lakh crore. But it's already November and we know that recovery is eluding us and the process may take longer. Till then the banking system will starve for capital.

According to RBI October to December report, the gross NPAs of PSBs are just under Rs 4 lakh crore, and they collectively account for 90% of such rotten apples in the country's banking portfolio. In terms of net NPAs, their share is even higher—at 92% of the total bad loans reported so far in the banking system.

Indian Business Case Studies. V P Pawar, Bhagyashree Kunte, and Srinivas Tumuluri, Oxford University Press.
© ASM Group of Institutes, Pune, India 2022. DOI: 10.1093/oso/9780192869388.003.0009

What is NPA?

- The assets of the banks which don't perform (that is—don't bring any return) are called NPA or bad loans. Bank's assets are the loans and advances given to customers. If customers don't pay either interest or part of principal or both, the loan turns into bad loan.
- According to RBI, terms loans on which interest or instalment of principal remains overdue for a period of more than 90 days from the end of a particular quarter is called an NPA.
- However, in terms of agriculture/farm loans; the NPA is defined as under—for short duration crop agriculture loans such as paddy, Jowar, Bajra, etc. if the loan (instalment/interest) is not paid for two crop seasons, it would be termed as an NPA. For long duration crops, the above would be one crop season from the due date.

The Case Background

Banking industry is in bad shape in the country where the capital is becoming insufficient to meet the growing demands. The reason is rise in NPA's due to which if calculated properly almost all the PSBs have to shut down the shop. Basel accord has prescribed capital norms but the banks' position is far from reality. The government has taken decision to induce funds but in reality the funds are nowhere sufficient for banks to come out of the red. Why has this situation arisen and which sectors are contributing for the same?

How Grim Is the Situation?

- According to the RBI's statistical tables relating to banks in India 2015–2016, NPAs were 3% of gross advances of all banks in India in 2013.
- By 2016, they had grown to 9.3%. The increase was much more pronounced for nationalized banks—from 2.9% in 2013 to 13.8% in 2016—compared to privately owned banks where the NPAs rose from 2% of gross advances in 2013 to 3.1% in 2016.

- For the 10 worst PSBs, gross NPAs averaged 16.4% of gross advances as on December 2016, from 22.4% for the Indian Overseas Bank to 14.1% for the Central Bank of India—in effect, each having thoroughly destroyed its balance sheet.
- The system does not have enough capital to take care of its bad loans.

What Possibly Led to This Situation?

- In an exuberant milieu that started with the UPA government and continued until three years after the global financial crisis of 2008, large corporations conceived major projects proposals in capital-intensive sectors such as power, ports, airports, housing, and highway construction.
- Banks were only too keen to lend, often without sufficient evaluation of risks and returns.
- Things started worsening with the policy paralysis brought about by the spectrum and coal mining scandals.
- Soon, most projects were getting stuck, especially in power and highways; and banks found their loans going sour.
- Initially, the extent of NPAs was hidden by 'ever-greening'. They were revealed as the RBI tightened the norms.

The Path Followed

It is significant that capital is being infused into banks. This could give the banking system a good breathing time to enhance its credit portfolio and restore value out of the NPA accounts. We may have to watch the situation unfolding over the next three years. During this time, the regulator, banks, and the government will have to focus on the quality of public sector banking assets, the NPAs, and the recovery. There has been a broad-brush approach to the quality assessment. The system will have to conduct more analysis, more evaluation sector-wise in terms of its potential for value restoration and enhancement. They will have to understand which sector is in a position to restore more economic value in six to eight quarters. Some sectors may perhaps take longer.

The last thing the economy and the banking system can afford is a further drop in economic value. What may be perceived as Rs 8 lakh crore problems today might grow into a much larger amount. The quality of governance will play a significant role in this regard. There has not been any worthwhile effort on this, unfortunately. There will have to be more reforms to put a higher order of governance in the banking sector. Ensuring performing boards at public-sector banks do become more critical. The last point which is equally important is that as long as the government wants to hold on to 51% equity in PSBs we cannot have a periodic injection by way of recaps bonds.

To fund the economy, the government will have to make a yearly budgetary allocation of the amount of capital required by PSBs. Programmes such as Indradhanush and small budgetary allocations will not work. The PSBs need budgetary allocation of at least Rs 75,000–80,000 crore each year.

The announcement of a stimulus into PSBs has been apparently understood as a bounty for the banks. An atmosphere is being projected that the government has been too generous to the banks and is serious about helping them to resolve the bad loans crisis. The quantum of capitalization announced leads one to believe so. In reality, this will not enable banks to recover the alarmingly huge bad loans which is the main issue confronting them.

Stressed Assets

The total stressed assets, bad loans, and restructured loans in banks are in the region of Rs 15 lakh crore. Instead of taking tough action on defaulters, the government came out with a 'novel scheme' to foist insolvency and bankruptcy proceedings on defaulters. This measure is not going to result in the recovery of bad loans. That is why the RBI has asked PSBs to be prepared for a deep haircut, up to 50% of the dues. Recently, on one account, a bank managed to recover just 6% of the total loan amount of Rs 950 crore. On 12 accounts, the dues are Rs 2.5 lakh crore. One can only imagine the additional provisions banks will have to make this year. There are more skeletons in the cupboard.

The Reality

There is a rush to 'punish' corporate culprits. The fact is that this is not a punishment, rather it is a reward. The defaulter promoter can himself bid before the IBC proceedings. Obviously, he is likely to be the highest bidder. So, he will retain his company but will have to shell out less than what he borrowed. This is legal innovation to pay less. But in the bargain, banks will lose huge amounts. One can safely predict that all banks will be running into losses by the end of the current financial year. Last year, while the gross operating profits were Rs 1,58,982 crore, after provisions for bad loans (Rs 1,70,370 crore), the net loss was Rs 11,388 crore. This year, it is bound to be worse. The IBC is only a ploy to extend favours to big corporates to escape from their liability at the cost of the public exchequer. Now let us see whether the recap announced by the finance minister will help PSBs, labelled as inefficient and incompetent. If banks would have recovered these loans, their interest revenue would have been more; income levels higher, profits high and they would have generated capital internally out of the profit. That door is closed because banks cannot recover loans through the IBC route. Thus, the banks' capital gets eroded and the capital adequacy ratio (CAR) becomes adverse.

Effects of Inadequate Capital

If banks do not have adequate capital, they cannot lend. This would dampen the economy, which is already in the doldrums. Hence to bolster the economy, banks have to be advised to give more loans. To give more loans, more capital is essential. That is why the announcement on recapitalization.

In the last three years, banks have written off Rs 188287 crore. We have to bear in mind that when banks lose money or when the government recapitalizes PSBs, it is all people's money and out of public savings kept in trust in the banks. People's money should be for people's welfare and not to fund corporate default or to recapitalize the banks to adjust these bad loans. The decision by the government to further capitalize PSBs is a welcome move. But does it really solve the problem of the lack of capital adequacy of PSBs? Let us examine.

Effects of NPA's

The problem of hidden bad assets is pervasive across the entire banking system. Both public and private sector banks are part of the story. If one bank had been undertaking fraudulent accounting practices and hiding problems, it could have been blamed, and its management punished, as in the case of Satyam and the conviction of Ramalinga Raju. If the problem was limited to PSBs, we would have found solutions in their governance. Private banks have also been hiding bad assets. The present NPA crisis appears to be as much a failing of the banking regulator. For many years, despite its unquestioned powers to regulate, supervise, and inspect banks, the regulator did not take action against banks that were hiding their bad assets. Instead, it proposed one loan restructuring scheme after another. None of the schemes, like CDR, SDR, and S4A, succeeded and stressed assets grew in number and value. It is only now, when credit growth has collapsed, that solving the problem cannot be postponed further and the regulator has become strict.

Regulatory failure across the world has led to changes in regulatory regimes, in laws, and in institutions. Creating checks and balances is a necessary element of the reform process. Independence and accountability are two sides of the same coin. Regulators must have both.

Conclusions

In the discussions about the reform that should accompany recapitalization, it is important to remember that it is not enough to reform PSBs. The problem of hiding NPAs is also present in private sector banks. The failures of banking regulation must be addressed and checks and balances created.

Case Questions

1. Majority of the NPAs are from the lending to few major groups of industries whose projects have either failed to take off or few them being in the gestation period for extending the initial projections. If

the problems are so severe as to badly affect the cash flows in major financial institutions calling for bailout packages from the government, how do you expect to approach the problem in terms of turnaround strategy for the banking industry in India?

2. With demands of farmers to waive off loans in many Indian states of huge amounts running into lakhs of crores of rupees and the government having no alternative other than accepting these demands—Is NPA going to be a regular impediment to economic progress of India? Besides each and every loan recovery case of Industry is getting in to NPAs and few of them resorting to running away from India to avoid punitive actions resulting government machinery getting occupied in bringing culprits to justice.

SECTION III

CASE STUDIES IN MULTIDISCIPLINARY AREAS IN MARKETING, STRATEGY, AND OPERATIONS

10

'Innovation and the Entrepreneurial Urge'

A Field Search Live Case Study on Creative Components Pvt Ltd MIDC Bhosari Pune

Learning Objectives

Indian entrepreneurs have played a key role in shaping the destiny of millions by providing them with jobs in their enterprises, venturing into untested arena and implementing innovative business strategies. It obviously draws our attention to case studies as to how Indian entrepreneurs succeed in their projects and the essence of such case study is that it can be used as a model for both emerging and aspiring entrepreneurs.

Synopsis

Entrepreneur is a human being, who conceives an industrial enterprise in his mind. To this end he makes tremendous efforts to put his vision to life. It is a purposive penetrating action to initiate, encourage, and control economic activity or practices for wealth creation and distribution. There should be an individual with a mind, heart, and purpose to combine them all and turn them into the production of the products and services people want. It is the entrepreneur who comes forward with the sole purpose of satisfying the customer by performing these production-related activities. A successful entrepreneur is always aware of the technological changes taking place in society around him and is prepared to adapt to the changing needs of society. He is the central point around whom all

Indian Business Case Studies. V P Pawar, Bhagyashree Kunte, and Srinivas Tumuluri, Oxford University Press.
© ASM Group of Institutes, Pune, India 2022. DOI: 10.1093/oso/9780192869388.003.0010

other factors of production, efficient resources, and techniques are to re-volve. He combines expertise, skills, and drives to turn the resources into successful ventures.

By acting as a bridge between creativity/innovation and the marketplace, entrepreneurship works as a productive factor in economic development more than just rising national income by generating new employment.

Case Facts

The enduring question of whether entrepreneurship is an inborn aptitude or a learned approach is still a mystery concealing the queuing of thou-sands of trained individuals to go to begging for secure employment. In most cases we see failures of entrepreneurial projects driven by compul-sions of friends and families based on either huge rewards and loans from financial institutions on favourable terms or pressure from corporations to outsource their requirements due to uncertainty of ROI in fresh invest-ments. The inherent supply chain efficiency pressure and intense market pace rivalry are throwing up millions of technology and e-commerce challenges and opportunities for so-called start-ups. The complexity of meeting peak demands in terms of advanced technologies and sustain-able pricing and delivery speed while maintaining zero inventory over the past few years has forced many small and medium-sized units to shut down shops.

Entrepreneurs—Take the Bull by the Horn Attitude

Yet there are few exceptions to the rule book among innovative entrepre-neurs who love challenges and changes and take the bull by the horn atti-tude embedded in their entrepreneurial characteristics. It was during one of our searches for these entrepreneurs during our academic field studies that we were fortunate to meet MR Ravi Hiremath, the 'No Nonsense' style entrepreneur, who gets nervous when it comes to learning.

Mr Ravi Hiremath is not a new entrant entrepreneur (prefers to be ad-dressed as Ravi). Ravi has been looking for challenges since his school and college days and has established his overall personality equipped with the necessary knowledge and exposure to uncertain business ways in the Indian industry and especially in the automotive sector in constant turmoil over regulatory compliance and audacious technological change in product, process, and marketing functions.

After his initial stay in a few manufacturing units to gain adequate insights into the manufacturing aspects, Ravi embarked on his endless spirited journey of entrepreneurial venturing and in 1996 formed a very small unit in a rented shed (300 sqft) to meet the tool maintenance re-quirements of a few major automotive mobile companies in Pune. The initial capital he was able to afford was mere Rs 5 lakhs including bor-rowing from friends and relatives to pay the rent and operating charges of his machine repair operations that had to endure longer credit period given to clients.

The Test of Uncertain Times

The 'Creative Components Pvt Ltd' Business launched today by pro-moters Mr Ravi and Mr Subhash Jaisinghani and Mr Shekhar Ballurgi as CEO stands as testimony to the grit. Fighting strength and innovative en-ergies of Ravi the managing director who feels proud to look back and de-scribe the test of uncertain times he successfully endured and scaled from a few thousand rupees per month to staggering Rs 20 crores turn over in 2017–2018 and aiming to reach the 30 crore mark in the next 2–3 years with an additional unit coming up at MIDC Chakan.

The Track Record 1996–2004

Creative metal crafts a collaboration company founded by Ravi after in-itial investment and expertise in tool and mould design added manu-facturing work to develop and supply prototype and batch form specifications for major customers such as Tata & M&M Ltd.

Throughout this time, the unit added basic manufacturing facilities such as heavy-duty press and plastic moulding machines with a capacity of 50–60 tons to its existing capacity in the manufacture of cast iron components and forged components needed for the manufacture and testing of tools.

The company reformulated itself in 2004 as Creative Components Pvt Ltd progressing from partnership established a Pvt Ltd setup with few more investors expressing confidence in the growth of Creative Components.

As of 2010–2011 Creative Components has established itself under Ravi's close guidance and leadership as an end to end model supplier of sub-assemblies to major automotive industries. Ravi's built customer loyalty through its tenacity to meet all of its customers' urgent and typical requirements has rendered Creative Components an indispensable tier1 supplier to major car giants in Maharashtra as well as other parts of India including MNCs.

Our team's unique observation while visiting Innovative Components was the overall operating area layout assisted by highly scientific material movement through the production assembly lines strictly following the Kan Ban Logistics Method maintaining JIT Inventory Management system. The coding method as seen and explained by Ravi is so good, that with minimal rejections and scrap traceability is extremely simple.

Consumer experiences are another special feature. All customer representatives have direct access to speak with Creative Component's design, production, assembly, and testing engineers. In fact, much of the assembly and testing of designing, process planning at Creative Components is finalized together with the Customer Engineers in order to ensure performance and 100% commitment to plan delivery. CEO Mr Bellaguri spends nearly 75% of his time with customer engineers to ensure that customer orders are met satisfactorily and to establish stronger working relationships with all customers. With this interaction nothing crops up as hurdles and botheration in smooth conduct of business.

The Organizational Structure

Creative components Pvt Ltd believes in teamwork and decentralized operational set-up. Except for external communications and technical specifications, there are divisions and organizational parts and customer-specific areas such as press shop, machine design, and production assembly and testing and, of course, an autonomous quality control system.

The company does not believe in regular internal meetings and problems are addressed electronically in the organizational sections TQM standards are successfully applied to ensure consistent work practices in each organizational area. The accountability, for productivity, quality, and schedule adherence is assigned to concerned cross-functional teams variances if any are discussed and recalibrated instantly.

The watchwords of Creative Components OSPs are multi-skilling and multi-task. Instead of system breakdowns, operations are rarely permitted to falter by proactive maintenance and multi-skilling in turn helps override occasional system operators absence. Issue resolution is handled through flexibility due to team level targets and team working. The open business activities mean that there is no Employees Union.

The Product

Major components of automotive applications in terms of hardware and mouldings subassemblies including sheet metal components of dashboard A/C systems, manifolds. Locks and locking systems are the key items on which Innovative Components have built their ability to supply highly competitive quality goods and delivery schedules based on JIT.

The Process

Creative's main equipment and machinery consists of high precision machining and electronic measurement devices including 3D CMM and subassembly of heavy-duty moulding machines and test equipment. Based on their business plans, Creative Components have plans for modernization and expansion.

The management Creative Components is aware of the current disruptive changes in the auto industry and is rigorously working out on future brand and marketing strategies and are ready to take the bull by the horn by penetrative consumer analysis and participation in to the future technology projects with all the major customers to understand and prepare for future eventualities due to technological and regulatory changes.

The Market

Nonetheless, as explained, creative components are among the first-tier suppliers to many of its customers due to variations in specifications and sophistication there are few more rivals for creative components with proprietary capacities and locational advantages and operational conveniences and at times due to changes in product specs requiring specialized production facilities. Creative Components are expected to meet approximately 15% of market requirements.

The Strategic Plans

Creative Components is preparing itself with its eyes and ears open to broader signals of radical changes in automobile design and operational technologies. Creative Components engineers are deputed on a regular basis to visit major auto exhibitions in India and abroad to study displayed model designs as well as to attend auto industry related conferences and seminars.

It is also necessary for Creative Components to reduce their dependence on the market in the automotive sector and to diversify into other areas such as white goods and railway and defence requirements that are now being opened up for small and medium-sized industries.

The Challenges

The main challenge for innovative parts, however, is the ongoing technical developments in the automotive industry. Because of the emission control and hybridization of auto designs and the use of renewable energy sources such as electric vehicles and drivers with fewer cars and transport vehicles, due diligence must be given to evolving regulatory standards, the future seems very hazy and uncertain in terms of OE requirements on the existing capabilities of Creative Components.

It is at times frightening to imagine over 10–15 years as to what would happen in automobile industry locally and internationally which can make existing skills and investment obsolete.

Conclusions

Entrepreneurship is about opportunity identification, development, and capture. This is the be-all and end-all. This is what entrepreneurs do and why they are called so. What separates most of us from successful entrepreneurs is that they are willing to spend the time and energy to go through this process. The process is not magic; it can be learnt. A clear discipline is involved in turning an idea into an opportunity. Companies which wish to rekindle their entrepreneurial spirit need to create an environment in which managers become impassioned about an idea to the point that they are willing to pursue it even if there are obstacles.

Case Questions

1. What would you asses as the short-term and long-term growth and risk patterns for Creative Components Pvt Ltd?

2. Creative components have been making huge investments in terms of plant and machinery for the current market requirements where there is enough potential for growth. However the looming regulatory controls in terms of pollution control norms as also the deglobalization plans of major markets for automobiles (America first) and related products in countries such as USA and UK (Brexit Effect) including Australia are likely to choke future investments in India by major MNCs leading to exodus of MNCs from India (already GM and Ford have announced curbing of future investments in India). Under these situations of turbulence in marketplace, what is your critical and distinct advice for the success of future plans of Creative Components Pvt Ltd.?

3. The EV onslaught as projected and reported in global news is likely
    to be the most disruptive for the auto industry. It is reported that
    by 2025–2030 the world is likely to see nearly 75% of the automo-
    biles in the EV version (which would need only 18–20 components
    below the bonnet compared nearly 250–300 of engine and trans-
    mission components alone including EMS).

    This even if it happens say around 50% of projections in India
    all the auto ancillaries will be worst affected. Creative Components'
    bread and butter today is the automobile sector. What is your re-
    commended strategy for Creative Components to survive the crisis
    and maintain business growth?

11

Chasing the 'Long Tail'

A Case Study on Long Tail Marketing Strategy

Learning Objectives

To evaluate the long tail marketing strategy and its applications. To analyse the effects of online retailing at the advent of Covid-19, the challenges and threats that the fixed retailers face. To analyse the change in e-commerce due to the increase in online retailing. To analyse the supply and demand on various products, their availability, customer satisfaction, and sales.

Synopsis

E-commerce involves the transaction of goods and services, the transfer of funds, and the exchange of data. It draws on technologies like mobile commerce, electronic funds transfer, supply chain management, internet marketing, and online transaction processing. In recent days, on sudden, unexpected advent of Covid-19, e-commerce has reached a higher place in the world of digitalization. This case study highlights online shopping versus traditional marketing. It also highlights the products which were of less importance and less in demand by consumers until the Covid-19 pandemic situation, gained more demand by young entrepreneurs to showcase their products on online retailing marketplaces.

The spread of online retailing has spawned many internet entrepreneurs hawking obscure or regionally known products. So when is the long tail market viable?

India's e-commerce story is no longer limited to billion-dollar valuations and discount-crazy consumers thronging shopping websites. The

Indian Business Case Studies. V P Pawar, Bhagyashree Kunte, and Srinivas Tumuluri, Oxford University Press.
© ASM Group of Institutes, Pune, India 2022. DOI: 10.1093/oso/9780192869388.003.0011

online marketplace has now become an incubator for entrepreneurs who are hawking rare, obscure, or even unpopular products. The shift was inevitable. The search for differentiation in an environment of cut-throat price competition has taken marketplaces like Snapdeal, Myntra, Pepperfry, and Fashionara to the doorstep of many small, regional brands, and makers of niche products, who are now able to sell their products across the country without worrying about managing logistics or marketing. Says Sandeep Komaravelly, senior vice-president, Marketing, Snapdeal, 'The online platform enables this transaction between sellers and buyers at zero upfront cost, and hence, the size of the business is not a pre-condition. This is how the online marketplace model democratizes entrepreneurism and business growth by giving people more options.'

So while analysts continue to question the sustainability of a model-driven by heavy discounting, some marketplaces are already chasing the long tail, tapping demand that is unarticulated and translating it into incremental sales. And since the internet makes distribution easier and uses state-of-the-art recommendation techniques to help consumers become aware of more obscure products, niches that weren't popular are now being discovered by consumers.

The simple truth is the long tail makes little economic sense in a physical world because stores only have so much shelf space and any brand/product stocked needs to justify its presence on the shelves by selling a requisite amount. On the other hand, it costs a Snapdeal nothing to put a rare, not-really-top-of-mind product on its catalogue, and sell a couple every week. Sure, it may never become a smash hit, but some sales in the long tail do add up to a significant market size.

In that sense, e-commerce has the potential to queer the pitch for the short head—large-volume, mass market products. Says Sudhir Voleti, assistant professor, Marketing, ISB, 'The long-tail model is about finding demand that is latent and players who find this latent demand will succeed.'

Product Is the Hero

At the end of the day, says Ganesh Subramanian, COO, Myntra, the hero of this story is the product, which is offered at a good price. He believes online platforms are a great opportunity for sellers since young buyers are willing to experiment. 'In terms of value, a third of our business comes from small-and medium-sized brands. We help with marketing support but success hinges on the product,' he says adding that while building scale to keep pace with growing demand can be tricky for a small producer, it is not impossible—one of his regional partners, for instance, has scaled Rs 50 Crores in revenue in two years.

Indeed, there are many such stories of internet entrepreneurs who ditched their jobs to sell fun products online. Some started for a lark, but now have credible businesses and are now building scale. Rahul Khullar, CEO and founder, Style Homez Inc, for instance, decided to sell bean bags from his home in 2013 in Delhi. His relationship with Snapdeal began in November 2013. From 30–40 pieces a month, Khullar now sells 3,200 pieces. Says Khullar, 'We grew 100 times in one year and the branding support that Snap deal provided through newspaper inserts and via Google ads drew customers to our website and urged them to check out our products.' The brand today services more pin codes in the country than it had hoped for in 2013. The team has also grown and stands at 35 people right now.

Anupam Barman, a silk sari retailer based in Varanasi, has seen his sales jump 25% in 2014 compared to the previous year, after Snapdeal approached him to sell his products on the portal. Not only has Barman found a new audience for his woven silks, he now gets to connect with the consumers directly and gets feedback on what products sell well and which ones require a bigger push.

Khullar of Style Homez says that since his venture was self-funded, it did not have the required financial muscle to invest in brand building. But its relationship with Snapdeal gave it instant visibility. What has worked to his advantage is the payments cycle, which coincides with a sale.

Kitsch Is the King

One visible trend is that most marketplaces are reaching out to people who either manufacture or deal in kitschy products. Arun Sirdeshmukh, founder of Fashionara, says unusual products that are not found in physical stores do well on online channels. Unusual gift items or trinkets are known to attract millennials who tend to shop more frequently online.

Given that most of these merchants are not really bred-in-the-bone merchants they need support in product selection and in showcasing them online. Most marketplaces help merchants build their e-catalogue and in listing them on the platform. In many cases even the product descriptions and photoshoots are facilitated by the e-commerce platform. Even when it comes to inventory management, the shopping portals give inputs to the sellers on the minimum inventory they need to hold at any given point in time according to the category. Akshay Juneja, founder of Fabdeal, an ethnic wear brand from Surat that sells on Myntra, says that Myntra gives his team a heads-up on how their stock is doing and how many pieces of which design they should they hold. Says Juneja, 'The advantage of this relationship is global reach. When we were offline we could only sell to local customers; now we reach overseas audience as well. From 50 pieces a day, our sales have gone up to 200–300 pieces a day'. During the festive season, Fabdeal had to organize delivery of 600 pieces a day. 'That said, some analysts are wary of the long tail theory's implicit challenge to the Pareto principle—or the so-called 80–20 rule, which would make it appear that there was a greater importance of the hit products'—and warn the long tail theory may not be universally applicable. In a working paper titled, 'Is Tom Cruise Threatened? Using Netflix Prize Data to Examine the Long Tail of Electronic Commerce', Wharton Operations and Information Management professor Serguei Netessine and doctoral student, Tom F Tan contended that while the long tail effect holds true in some cases, mass appeal products retain their importance when expanding product variety and consumer demand are factoring in.

'There are companies based on the premise of the Long Tail effect that argue they will make money focusing on niche markets,' says Netessine. 'Our findings show it is very rare in business that everything is so black and white. In most situations, the answer is, "It depends." The presence of the Long Tail effect might be less universal than one may be led to believe.'

According to Netessine, 'The Long Tail effect may be present in some cases, but few companies operate in a pure digital distribution system. Instead, they must weigh supply chain costs of physical products against the potential gain of capturing single customers of obscure offerings. Companies must also consider the time it takes for consumers to locate off-beat items they may want. Also the task before the curated marketplaces is far from easy. They have to evaluate the products for their quality and the vendor for his reliability to be able to make a difference in the market'.

Most of the marketplaces have separate quality teams to monitor products, quality, and catalogue. Mind you, this is not a one-time effort but has to be done continuously. That apart, the onus of distribution also lies with the marketplace. On receiving an order a marketplace will connect with the relevant vendor and take care of the packaging and delivery within the promised time. Managing reverse logistics—ferrying returned products—is also handled by the concerned marketplace.

Handholding new entrepreneurs might be a wonderful thing and the long tail might earn e-commerce players rich dividends, but is the model sustainable? Most sellers on these marketplaces are growing at breakneck speed and if this growth continues, they will have to scale up rapidly to meet demand. Failure to meet demand or quality expectations would not only harm the vendor, it has the potential to hurt the credibility of the marketplace as well. Fashionara's Sirdeshmukh, however, does not believe it is an issue. Most marketplaces use advanced predictive analytics to get a sense of future demand. If they sense that a vendor cannot meet the demand, the easiest thing to do is to remove the vendor's catalogue from the site. Subramanian of Myntra says, 'The growth of these smaller brands will be determined by their ability to scale up. They have to invest in infrastructure.'

Most e-commerce portals believe that this trend will play out in two ways. Some of these brands will emerge as strong standalone brands in their own right. If and when they do, they would want to migrate to their own websites. On the other hand, some will remain niche and only cater to an audience their inventory allows them to service. However, maintaining quality and managing the time-to-consumer-doorstep will continue to be the biggest challenges on their way.

Conclusions

E-commerce provides multiple benefits to the consumers in form of availability of goods at lower cost, wider choice, and saves time. Many young entrepreneurs have opted for online retailing reaching the vendors of unpopular products. Online retail marketplace has now become the most sought destination by the entrepreneurs for constant profitable products. The products which were less known and less in demand as well, until the Covid pandemic situation.

Case Questions

1. Explain how can long tail theory of marketing be achieved in post corona pandemic situation? Give examples.

2. What are the factors that influence the steady revenue from less demand products and at the same time catering to the need of the consumers?

3. Explain the applications of long tail theory of marketing strategy.

12

The Price of Owning a 'Cheetah' (The Jaguar)

'A Case Study in International Acquisition Growth Strategy' (Tata-JLR)

Learning Objectives

To understand how valuation of brand is done in international market. To know more about the international environmental factors affecting profitability of the firm. To understand the concept of economics of scale and its impact on financial health of an organization. To know more about merger and acquisition strategy of business expansion in international market. To understand financial implications of merger and acquisition. To know, what is the right time to acquire an international firm? To understand the importance of synergies among merging organization for success of the merger.

Synopsis

This case study discusses the acquisition of herculean automobile giant JLR by an Indian automobile company Tata motors. Prior acquisition by Ford motors, Jaguar and Land Rover were owned by British multinational automobile company, 'British Leyland'. Ford first acquired Jaguar brand in 1983 for $2.5 billion and then Land Rover 2000 for $2.7 billion brand from British Leyland.

In spite of multiple attempts, Ford motors recorded heavy losses due to these two brands. The losses continued until these two brands were

Indian Business Case Studies. V P Pawar, Bhagyashree Kunte, and Srinivas Tumuluri, Oxford University Press.
© ASM Group of Institutes, Pune, India 2022. DOI: 10.1093/oso/9780192869388.003.0012

acquired by Indian automobile giant Tata motors in 2008 for just $1.7 billion. Many critics felt that Ford motors is the biggest loser in this merger deal. On the other hand some critics are also of opine that, Tata motors will also be on the losing side. They feel that, though Tata motors are in the entry-level passenger car segment, there expertise is in heavy load goods vehicles. They feel that what Ford could not achieve in 20 years, it is impossible for inexperienced Tata motors in globally acceptable luxury passenger car market.

It was in early 2008 that the attention of many involved in Indian auto industry was focused on the issue of a major merger deal happening between the iconic 'Jaguar & Land Rover—JLR', A division of the Ford motor company of USA and the Indian giant 'TATA MOTORS'. For many stalwarts around the world this was quite an intriguing development, since there was no obvious synergy between the two units. Ford was the global giant in the design, development of passenger cars of global iconic value over the previous 8 decades and had spent nearly 20 years in trying to resurrect life in to the ailing Jaguar brand of high-end sedans, and the workhorse models under the Rover brand of SUVs. Whereas the Indian Tata's have been in the truck manufacturing business since the early 1900 till 1998 when they ventured in to the manufacture of a small car 'Indica' a fully homegrown product without much of global iconic image. In fact Tata's themselves call as a cheap car meant for the Indian customers and the Indian roads, both calling for major compromises in drivability, and customer comforts. This merger proposal, therefore, appeared like a bout between a harassed 'sumo wrestler' and a small city circus artist.

Ford motor company acquired the Jaguar brand in 1983 for $2.5 billion, and the Land Rover of r$2.7 billion in 2000 and clubbed the two in its Premier Automotive Group (PAG), along with its other models Aston Martin and the Volvo Cars. This move of Ford motors was basically aimed at countering the strong move by the Toyotas to enter the US market with their Lexus model for the luxury car segment. As expected the Toyota's unveiling their Lexus LS400 in 1980 in the US markets made a huge impact shaking every American player in the segment. This forced Ford motor company to acquire the Jaguar in spite of comparatively higher acquisition price. The Jaguar model had a head on competition with the famous BMW and Mercedes Benz and was already a failing proposition since, even in 2007 the sales of Jaguar were a mere 60,000 numbers against BMW's 1.6 million and Merc's 1.3 million. The Jaguar model from the beginning suffered due to its high cost and low volumes. There was no alternative than to pump in huge money in to new product development, but as disasters won't wait for long the heart-breaking rejection of the X-Type model by the customers who expected Jaguar to perform far better than its competition. The sales realizations from the X-Type Jaguar were 10% of the estimates at its best.

The Land Rover story was slightly better in the sense that it had sold nearly 2.25 million vehicles in 2007, and was a preferred brand for the four-wheel drive SUVs. But Land Rover also needed fresh investment for the up-gradation required for the new emission rules compliance. Land Rover also needed substantial investments for the development of the hybrid technology in its range of vehicles. Ford spent nearly $400 million for this purpose on the Land Rover model. Land Rover vehicles also needed to fix some serious quality problems since on annual initial *Quality survey* it was at the bottom of the list. Besides all this Jaguar and Land Rover vehicles had failed to impress buyers in the US and the Asian markets.

The Tata's Status

The Tata's were in the commercial vehicle segment for nearly 60 years and the passenger car segment has been a very recent territory they have entered in late 1990's. In view of the new product for an altogether new customer profile, Tata's have faced major performance quality problems in the small car segment, and only towards 2005 they have been able to lick all these niggling problems, and have introduced the Sedan version of the Indica also simultaneously upgrading the base model Indica to the V2 and the Vista model which have established a fair amount of confidence in its customers, however they still lack their competition in terms of customer satisfaction levels and the niggling product quality issues. There exists a limitation up to which the Tata's can stretch their capability in the indigenous design and development of cars for the luxury car segment. The Tata's therefore were shopping for an opportunity to acquire world-class design, development, and manufacturing capability for cars in the high-end luxury segment. This is when the Ford JLR proposal came up for takeover.

Everyone including few executives in Tata's was in for a major surprise when the takeover of the iconic brands of the 'Jaguar and Land Rover Brands' by Tata at a very high financial outlay of $2.3 billion towards the acquisition. This the Tata group was definitely not in a position to afford from its own funds and need to borrow, especially in view of it's the huge funds it had raised for the acquisition of Corus Steel and Co. by a group company the Tata steel for $12.3 billion. There were serious apprehensions and criticisms, from all corners of the world towards this massive merger the Tata's had decided. One could not see any business opportunity for the Tata's at least for the next 10 years in view of the huge technological gap between Tata's and the JLR, and that the background of the world-class Ford motor company failing to revive JLR in the past 20 years. There appeared nothing so great in Tata's capability which could be far better than that of the Fords. Besides around this time Tata motor's main division the commercial vehicles including the passenger car were accumulating losses in view of the decline in the global automobile markets. However the takeover deal was concluded in early 2008.

Critical Appraisal of the Takeover of JLR by Tata Motors

For the Ford Motors

1) The critics felt that Ford motors is the biggest loser in the deal. As against the initial payment of $5.0 billion while acquiring the JLR, Ford had spent several billion in its revival efforts for the iconic models of JLR. It had also invested heavily in the R&D infrastructure for new models of Jaguar and Land Rover. As against this it was getting only $1.7 billion from the deal after adjusting for the pension deficit.

2) The business analysts felt that in bargain, Ford was getting a pittance of $1.7 billion was in no way improving the liquidity situation

for Ford. They felt that at least by delaying the deal for some more time to recover some of its investments made in new products such as the Jaguar XF and LR2 which could have revived the markets for them.

3) With this deal, Ford also will stand to lose the annual royalty payments to the tune of 126 million pounds from Land Rover all its financial resources. And the losses on Jaguar had eaten away. At the end of the day Ford has got a very raw deal.

For Tata Motors Ltd

1) The experts feel that this deal is going to hit the finances of Tata motors very adversely. Besides a massive bridge loan for $2.3 billion, they will need to service an interest burden of $30.0 billion per quarter. This will burgeon in to a steep rise in the annual losses and will definitely affect its market capitalization very severely. (Immediately after the takeover deal announcement Tata motors shares crumbled down by a massive 6%.) The rating agencies also have downgraded the Tata scripts and moved in to negative implications.

2) Unless there is a revival in the market acceptance of Jaguar new models there is not going to be any benefit to the Tata's from this deal. Besides the serious quality problems on the Land Rover and compliance to new emission norms which call for additional and immediate investments will further drain the financial muscles of the Tata's which are already overburdened.

3) The design and manufacturing infrastructures at JLR are for quite some time likely to be beyond the reach of Tata's domestic expertise. Excepting for management supervision and pursuing the Ford for continued help in the design and development of new models for Jaguar, Tata's current core competence will be of little use in the revival attempts for JLR. (It is understood that the deal specifies a contract with the Ford to continue supplies of engines for the Jaguar model for three more years till JLR has its own capacity increase as required.)

People basically disbelieve, that what the mighty Fords could not achieve in 20 years, Tata's with literally no experience in globally acceptable luxury passenger car markets, will be able to turn around JLR and make profits for which Fords burnt their fingers in spite of being one of great three auto manufacturers. Hence this deal is likely to be a millstone around the neck of the Tata group for a very long time.

Where Are the Synergies?

There is great amount of apprehension in the minds of the experts as also the common man, in respect of the synergies between the Indian Tata's and the Iconic JLR. Tata's even today are considered as manufacturers of the famous Tata trucks which occupy major roads in India for goods transport. The common man while appreciating Tata's daredevil entry in to the passenger car segments still feels Tata's cannot make world-class luxury cars because of their basic mindset of manufacturing trucks. The very fact that many foreign car manufacturers like the Hyundai, Toyota, Skoda, GM, BMW are leaders in the growing passenger car market (not to forget the Indian Maruti Suzuki cars) in the luxury car segment and Tata's are nowhere in this segment gives doubts to feel that one day Tata's Jaguar cars will be seen on the Indian roads as well.

Even in the global markets, in spite of the pioneering global marketing expertise of the Ford motors, over the past 20 years, Jaguar cars have failed to attract customers in the biggest markets for luxury cars, the US and the Asian countries. How could one expect that Tata's who do not have any representation in the global markets for the luxury passenger cars would be able to penetrate new markets leave alone maintaining same impact as the Fords in the existing markets. On the contrary Tata's as the new owners of JLR are likely to face negative remarks on their capability to provide leadership in the marketing and servicing of marquee brands like Jaguar and Land Rover.

Ford motors, excepting for the lower transaction price, are going to lose on their regular royalty income from Land Rover. Besides this deal may work out as setback since it has failed to resurrect JLR, in spite of heavy investments and new model failures of Jaguar. Besides they are required to settle the outstanding pension payments, and keep supplying engines to the new owner for three more years as per the settlement.

The cultural integration between, JLR employees, suppliers, customers, and Tata's is one more major issue on which Tata's will need to work hard.

The major issues on the technological front are the product improvement new model introduction for the Jaguar and resolution of the serious product quality problems on the Land Rover models, including compliance to new emission norms. In general the acquisition deal does not seem to offer many synergy benefits to both the parties post-acquisition.

The Ambiguities in the Deal

At the time of sealing the deal, the following aspects were not clear:

1. How much, and how long will Ford be required to help Tata JLR in servicing and warranty issues on the vehicles already on the roads? How long will Ford need to provide technical support to the new owner for the introduction of new models in the pipeline as also to supply engines for the regular production of the Jaguar cars?
2. How much of the accrued losses of JLR have Ford taken in its books? How big were these amounts? How was the figure of $ 2.3 billion arrived at since Tata was to take over a near debt-free JLR?
3. In a retrospective framework of recent developments Tata's seem to have been benefitted by the overall recovery in the global auto markets, mainly in view of the recovery in the global economical scenario. But JLR is likely to be an area calling for utmost prudence for a very long time on all fronts for the Tata's. Any turbulence in the markets is likely to throw the situation back to square ONE.

Case Questions

1. What is the strategic plan both in short and long terms for the Tata's to have invested so heavily in the acquisition of JLR from Ford?

2. Neither Tata's in India nor JLR worldwide are among the top few in the CSI (customer satisfaction index), in this context, do you think that Tata's will gain a competitive advantage out of this acquisition?

3. In the view of the heavy investments Tata's has made for acquiring JLR, suggest a business model for recovery of the capital investment.

13

Liar, Liar—Is 'Apple' on Fire?

A Case Study on Sustaining Competitive Advantage

Learning Objectives

To provide world with the best innovations and technologies in the world. To find out the success recipe for new product development and how companies make good advantage of the success recipe. Understanding the relation between culture and innovations. To ensure good health and safety of the company's employees, customers, and the global communities.

Synopsis

The New World Encyclopaedia (2018) states that Apple Inc., formerly Apple Computer, Inc., is a multinational corporation that creates consumer electronics, personal computers, servers, and computer software, and is a digital distributor of media content. The company also has a chain of retail stores known as Apple Stores. Apple's core product lines are the iPhone, iPod, and Macintosh computer. Founders Steve Jobs and Steve Wozniak created Apple Computer on 1 April 1976, and incorporated the company on 3 January 1977, in Cupertino, California.

For more than three decades, Apple Computer was predominantly a manufacturer of personal computers, including the Apple II, Macintosh, and Power Mac lines, but it faced rocky sales and low market share during the 1990s. Jobs, who had been ousted from the company in 1985, returned to Apple in 1996 after his company next was bought by Apple. The following year he became the company's interim CEO, which later became permanent. Jobs subsequently instilled a new corporate philosophy

Indian Business Case Studies. V P Pawar, Bhagyashree Kunte, and Srinivas Tumuluri, Oxford University Press.
© ASM Group of Institutes, Pune, India 2022. DOI: 10.1093/oso/9780192869388.003.0013

of recognizable products and simple design, starting with the original iMac in 1998.

With the introduction of the successful iPod music player in 2001 and iTunes Music Store in 2003, Apple established itself as a leader in the consumer electronics and media sales industries, leading it to drop 'Computer' from the company's name in 2007. The Company sells and delivers digital content and applications through the iTunes Store, App Store, Mac App Store, television APP Store, iBook's Store, and Apple Music (collectively Internet Services).

The Company sells its products through its retail stores, online stores, and direct sales force through third-party cellular network carriers, wholesalers, retailers, and value-added resellers. The Company sells a range of third-party Apple compatible products, including application software and accessories through its retail and online stores. The Company sells to consumers, small and mid-sized businesses and education, enterprise, and government customers.

Cloud is the Company's cloud service, which stores music, photos, contacts, calendars, mail, documents, and more, keeping them up-to-date and available across multiple iOS devices, Mac, and Windows personal computers and Apple TV. iCloud services include Drive, Photo Library, Family Sharing, Find My iPhone, iPad or Mac, Find My Friends, Notes, iCloud Keychain, and I Cloud Backup for iOS devices. AppleCare offers a range of support options for the Company's customers. The cult of Apple is strong. Or was it? Consumers are not happy. And when consumers are not happy, the survival of a company is in jeopardy and Apple is now being accused of programmed obsolescence.

Case Details

Bra shares (2001) tell us that Apple Computers, Inc. was founded on 1 April 1976, by college dropouts Steve Jobs and Steve Wozniak, who brought to the new company a vision of changing the way people, viewed computers. Jobs and Wozniak wanted to make computers small enough for people to have them in their homes or offices. Simply put, they wanted a computer that was user-friendly.

The two Steve's—Jobs and Wozniak—may have been Apple's most visible founders, but were it not for their friend Ronald Wayne there might be no iPhone, iPad, or iMac today. Jobs convinced him to take 10% of the company stock and act as an arbiter should he and Wozniak come to blows, but Wayne backed out 12 days later, selling for just $500 a holding that would have been worth $72bn 40 years later. Woz produced the first computer with a typewriter-like keyboard and the ability to connect to a regular TV as a screen. Later christened the Apple I, it was the archetype of every modern computer, but Wozniak wasn't trying to change the world with what he'd produced—he just wanted to show off how much he'd managed to do with so few resources.

Speaking to Byte magazine in December 1984, Woz credited Jobs with the idea. 'He was working from time to time in the orchards up in Oregon. I thought that it might be because there were apples in the orchard or maybe just its fruitarian nature. Maybe the word just happened to occur to him. In any case, we both tried to come up with better names but neither one of us could think of anything better after Apple was mentioned.'

According to the biography of Steve Jobs, the name was conceived by Jobs after he returned from Apple farm. He apparently thought the name sounded 'fun, spirited and not intimidating'. The name also likely benefitted by beginning with an A, which meant it would be nearer the front of any listings.

Apple and Microsoft

If it was a soap opera, Apple and Microsoft's on-off relationship would put many to shame. Today, you'd never guess there had ever been anything wrong, and that's probably down to the fact that their relationship has never been more symbiotic.

Weinberger tells fast forward to 1996, when Jobs appeared in a PBS documentary called 'Triumph of the Nerds' and just ripped into Gates and Microsoft, saying that they make 'third-rate products'. Jobs went on in that same documentary: 'The only problem with Microsoft is they just have no taste. They have absolutely no taste. And I don't mean that in a small way, I mean that in a big way, in the sense that they don't think of original ideas, and they don't bring much culture into their products.'

By 1997, Jobs was Apple CEO. At his first Macworld keynote, he announced that he had accepted an investment from Microsoft to keep Apple afloat. Bill Gates appeared on a huge screen via satellite uplink. The audience booed. Gates clearly admired Jobs, even if they didn't always see eye to eye. When Apple introduced iTunes, Gates sent an internal email to Microsoft that said 'Steve Jobs' ability to focus in on a few things that count, get people who get user interface right, and market things as revolutionary are amazing things.'

Wikipedia describes the movie 'Pirates of Silicon Valley' as an original 1999 American made for television biographical drama film, directed by Martin Burke and starring Noah Wyle as Steve Jobs and Anthony Michael Hall as Bill Gates. Spanning the years 1971–1997 and based on Paul Freiberg and Michael Swine's 1984 book Fire in the Valley: The Making of the Personal Computer, it explores the impact of the rivalry between Jobs (Apple Computer) and Gates (Microsoft) on the development of the personal computer.

Rozsa said that: 'unfortunately, there was a darker side to the PC revolution, which is why the word "Pirates" appears in the title of 'Pirates of Silicon Valley.' While Jobs and Gates were indisputably brilliant men, they did not invent much of the technology that is widely attributed to them.

No, the credit for those innovations belongs to countless obscure men and women—many of the employees at Xerox, which paid them to create marvels and then refused to make bank on their work because it didn't appreciate what they had. Jobs realized this and, characteristically, charmed Xerox into forcing its resentful employees to share the fruits of their labour's with the self-entitled Jobs, who thought nothing of harvesting their bounty and acting like he had cultivated it himself.

This brings us to the other scene that captures the essence of this movie's greatness, an exchange between Jobs and Gates after the former realizes the latter has been stealing his innovations (much as Jobs did to the hapless Xerox employees), which I dare not quote here for risk of spoiling it for others. Suffice to say this much: This is as much a film about intellectual theft, and the grandiose egotism necessary to morally justify such actions, as it is about genius and inspiration and the world-changing technology they wrought.

Burying the Hatchets

IDC figures released in summer 2015 showed Mac sales to have climbed by 16% over the previous quarter. At the same time, though, the overall PC market for machines running Windows had dipped by 11.8%. So, with ever more of Microsoft's revenue coming from Office 365, it needs to push its subscription-based productivity service onto as many platforms as it can—including Android, iOS, and, of course, the Mac.

Apple, on the other hand, needs Office. It has its own productivity apps in the shape of Pages, Numbers, and Keynote, but Word, Excel, and PowerPoint remain more or less industry standards, so if it's going to be taken seriously in the business world, Apple needs Microsoft Office on board.

So, a peace has broken out—and a long-lasting one at that, which despite some sniping from either side, stretches right back to Jobs' return to Apple after his time at the Nets (we'll come to that later), but suffice it to say at this point that it shouldn't really surprise us: the rivalry between the two camps often seems overblown. Microsoft developed many of the Office apps for the Mac before porting them to the PC and, in the early days at least.

Bill Gates had good things to say about the company. 'To create a new standard, it takes something that's not just a little bit different,' he said in 1984, 'it takes something that's really new, and really captures people's imagination. And the Macintosh—of all the machines I've seen—is the only one that meets that standard.'

That's pretty flattering, but there's a saying about flattery: imitation is its sincerest form. Apple apparently didn't see it that way when Microsoft, in Apple's eyes, went on to imitate its products a little too faithfully. As we already know, Apple had been inspired by certain elements of an operating system it saw at Xerox PARC when it was developing the Macintosh and Lisa. Xerox's implementation used the desktop metaphor now familiar to OS X, Windows, and many Linux users, and when Microsoft was developing Windows 1.0, Apple licensed some of its fundamentals to the company that Jobs latterly took to calling 'our friends up north'.

In 2014, Microsoft named its top cloud computing executive, Satya Nadella, as chief executive on. The Company also said Bill Gates would step aside as chairman of the board but would remain a technology adviser to the company. John Thompson, who has been the lead independent director, became chairman.

Nadella's appointment ends a longer-than-expected search for a new leader after Steve Ballmer the Microsoft former CEO, announced his intention to retire in August of 2013. Nadella is only the third CEO in Microsoft's 39-year history, following co-founder Bill Gates and Ballmer. Before Microsoft, the Indian-born executive worked at Sun Microsystems.

The famously ebullient Ballmer—who joined Microsoft in 1980 as the company's first business manager and rose quickly through the ranks—leaves the company after 13 difficult years as CEO. The company was once the most valuable in the world, but Microsoft has lost more than half of its market value over the past decade.

With Nadella, the tables have turned in the Microsoft-Apple rivalry. For decades, Apple had but a sliver of the market share for personal computers. In 2014, Apple was not only shipping more personal computers—counting the ones that fit in our pockets—it was making much more money from them. Apple made $156 billion in revenue from iPhones, iPads, and Macs in the last year. And Microsoft? Between Windows and Office software, Nokia phones and Surface tablets, it saw about $23 billion in revenue.

Steve Jobs Era

Apple's popularity exploded in the 2000s. The iPod, smaller and sleeker with each generation, introduced many lifelong Windows users to their first Apple gadget. The arrival of the iTunes music store in 2003 gave people a convenient way to buy music legally online, song by song. For the music industry, it was a mixed blessing. The industry got a way to reach Internet-savvy people who, in the age of Napster, were growing accustomed to downloading music free. But online sales also hastened the demise of CDs and established Apple as a gatekeeper, resulting in battles between Jobs and music executives over pricing and other issues.

Jobs' command over gadget lovers and pop culture swelled to the point that, on the eve of the iPhone's launch in 2007, faithful followers slept on sidewalks outside posh Apple stores for the chance to buy one.

Three years later, at the iPad's debut, the lines snaked around blocks and out through parking lots, even though people had the option to order one in advance.

Perhaps most influentially, Jobs in 2001 launched the iPod, which offered '1,000 songs in your pocket'. Over the next 10 years, its white earphones and thumb-dial control seemed to become more ubiquitous than the wristwatch.

In 2007 came the touch-screen iPhone, joined a year later by Apple's App Store, where developers could sell iPhone 'apps' which made the phone a device not just for making calls but also for managing money, editing photos, playing games, and social networking. And in 2010, Jobs introduced the iPad, a tablet-sized, all-touch computer that took off even though market analysts said no one really needed one.

By 2011, Apple had become the second-largest company of any kind in the United States by market value. In August, it briefly surpassed Exxon Mobil as the most valuable company. Under Jobs, the company cloaked itself in secrecy to build frenzied anticipation for each of its new products. Jobs himself had a wizardly sense of what his customers wanted, and where demand didn't exist, he leveraged a cult-like following to create it.

When he spoke at Apple presentations, almost always in faded blue jeans, sneakers, and a black mock turtleneck, legions of Apple acolytes listened to every word. He often boasted about Apple successes, then coyly added a code—'one more thing' before introducing its latest ambitious idea.

In later years, Apple investors also watched these appearances for clues about his health. Jobs revealed in 2004 that he had been diagnosed with a very rare form of pancreatic cancer—an islet cell neuroendocrine tumour. He underwent surgery and said he had been cured.

In 2009, following weight loss he initially attributed to a hormonal imbalance, he abruptly took a six-month leave. During that time, he received a liver transplant that became public two months after it was performed.

He went on another medical leave in January 2011, this time for an unspecified duration. He never went back and resigned as CEO in August, though he stayed on as chairman. Consistent with his penchant for secrecy, he didn't reference his illness in his resignation letter.

Post-Steve Jobs Era

Apple's creative director Hugh Dubberly was concerned that Apple is in danger of being left behind by Samsung now that the company is in the post-Steve Jobs era. Apple's biggest strategic mistake since Steve Jobs' death has been to concede the power-user market. Apple no longer makes anything that could be regarded as a high-end workstation. Apple has only the (trashcan) Mac Pro, which has been a bit of a disaster. That machine is too constrained to have general purpose utility.

The most powerful iMacs cannot support a desktop class GPU.

Nevertheless, Tim Cook is succeeding at an impossible task, following the greatest-ever product visionary as Apple's CEO. Yet six years after his mentor Steve Jobs died, Apple is thriving. And Cook is growing into his prominence as one of the business world's most increasingly vocal good-guy CEOs.

For Apple, 2017 was a return to growth. After sales declines in 2016, Apple has now posted four consecutive quarters of year-over-year revenue gains—and it's accelerating. The Apple Watch, the first major new product launched under the Cook era, has quietly become a big hit. Air Pods are amazing and exciting. Together, they form a wearable computer line up that has many interesting applications, notably fitness and medicine. Cook and company are also setting Apple up to succeed in augmented reality—where real life and computer graphics are mixed—which many see as one of the next big technology waves.

Apple has a group of loyal users in the academic community. It has loyal users in the visual effects community and loyal users in game development and VR. There are even a significant number of common-or-garden software developers, all of whom would gladly pay-out for a machine with lots of RAM, lots of cores, and a giant smoking GPU. But there is a problem: by not offering a suitable machine for these users, Apple has burned a pile of good will with its most influential (and wealthiest) customers.

In pure commercial terms, there is absolutely nothing wrong with this decision. The amount of actual revenue this market represents is less than a rounding error on Apple's bottom line. By dropping the top-end machines, Apple's engineers can focus on other products which really do generate profits. The return on investment for high-end workstations will be far less than phones, consumer computers or even watch bands.

The Criticism on Apple

In the last few years, Apple has been struggling with complaints from all over the world. India, France, Italy, South Korea, China, and this is just exploding. Apple is accused of much dubious behaviour. For instance, they have been claimed by critics to combine stolen and/or purchased designs that it claims are its own original creations; unethical business practices such as anti-competitive behaviour, rash litigation, and dubious tax tactics, their production methods involving the use of sweatshop labour, customer service issues involving misleading warranties and insufficient data security, and concerns about environmental destruction.

Additionally, it has been criticized for its alleged collaboration with US surveillance programme, PRISM. Later, they denied knowing about this issue. In YouTube, there are some short documentaries talking about how many workers from manufacturers for Apple, are getting cancer. It is related with benzene poisoning and how they develop occupational cancer.

But in spite of these awful situations, the slowdown of older iPhones is the most scandalous yet expensive complaint for Apple. Apple has accepted some responsibility of it and right now (2018) the company is trying to solve this situation. Apple acknowledged on December of 2017, that the iPhone software had the effect of slowing down some phones with battery problems, but denied that it had ever done anything to intentionally shorten the life of a product.

The firm apologized for its actions and cut battery replacement costs. It has also said it would change its software to show users whether their phone batteries were working well. On 28 December, Apple apologized, but nearly 67,000 iPhone users in Korea have applied to join a lawsuit against Apple as the company admitted to deliberately slowing down the performance of older models to prolong battery life.

At least 15 class action cases have been filed against Apple in the US and international markets. The one in France, which holds the potential of criminal charges, seems to be the most dangerous one, while the one in the US that asks for nearly a trillion dollars in damage is the funniest one. Lawsuits have been filed against Apple in California, New York, and Illinois alleging the company defrauded users by slowing down devices without warning.

The company also faces a legal complaint in France, where so-called planned obsolescence is against the law. Lomas mentions that programmed obsolescence is illegal in France under a 2015 law which prohibits 'the use of techniques by which the person responsible for the marketing of a product aims to deliberately reduce the duration to increase the replacement rate'. The law carries a penalty of a maximum sentence of two years in prison and up to 5% of a company's annual turnover.

However the firm said: 'We have never—and would never—does anything to intentionally shorten the life of any Apple product, or degrade the user experience to drive customer upgrades.'

Apple's Strategy to Re-Establish Customer's Satisfaction

In South Korea, Apple has said that as part of its next update, expected in March of 2018, it will give users the option to turn off the feature that slows down the older handsets. The firm has already reduced the price of any out-of-warranty iPhone 6 or later battery replacements, by more than half.

Ian Morris, a Forbes Media contributor explains: Firstly, Apple will replace the batteries in older phones for a greatly reduced price. The company will drop this service from $79 to $29. This will apply to anyone who has an iPhone 6 or later and will be available for the next year—ending in December 2018.

Secondly, the company says that it will provide more battery information from within iOS. This will give users a clear indication if it is the age of their battery that is causing them problems. For some users, it will simply be issues with apps. But the phone will make it clearer if a battery replacement would help or not.

The third step is to look at how Apple manages the phones themselves. If the customer had an unexpected shutdown then he/she might find that a less than ideal way for your phone to work. So perhaps in future, we'll see the iPhone sending notifications to warn that the battery in the device needs replacing. Or perhaps offering a choice of slowing down the max performance to get a bit more power—a bit like the existing power-saving mode.

The journalist Ramya Patel Khan made a quite interesting interview with David Temin, an RP consultant, and spoke about how Apple can restore trust and the crisis management. Davia Temin said Apple's explanation for the battery slowdown is 'perfectly adequate' but 'too little, too late'.

The explanation would've been acceptable before the issue arose or at the time of releasing updates that slowed devices. The explanation—forced by lawsuits, complaints, and information revealed by third parties—is inadequate. Temin says despite the bad software update process, very few users lost trust in Apple. However, when iPhone owners understood that the upgrades were planned to slow their devices, without even informing them, their trust just 'vanished'.

The problem began some time ago, but Apple didn't truthfully address it. It issued an apology on 28 December through a spokesperson only after lawsuits were filed. Temin said for restoring trust Apple should first 'revamp' the iPhone update process. She says users should be able to refuse updates; they shouldn't be forced or tricked into accepting updates. Before installation, users should be well-informed about what the update is for and the changes it brings.

Customers should have an option to undo or reverse an update if they don't like it.

Temin says Apple should get rid of 'defensiveness, arrogance, or radio silence' and instead communicates clearly and truthfully with customers in the time of crisis. Whenever an issue arises, Apple must address it immediately before it gets exposed 'by a third-party'.

Whenever there's public outrage about something, Apple should try and repair the situation before it gets worse. It must detect and respond to such situations before the damage is done or before law forces it.

Temin said Apple should start holding an 'on-going dialogue' with its users, adding the company should listen to people's concerns and then act on them. She also feels Apple must respond to every complaint it receives. She said Apple's associates, apart from those at support stations, must be empowered to send reports about the concerns or issues raised and also apologize when required. Also, the company must apologize 'early, sincerely, and without prompt or caveat'.

Davia Temin stated: 'Readjust your (Apple) global attitude. Give people a reason to love and trust you again . . . if you don't, your franchise will erode. Only your competitors want that, not the fan base that desperately wants to be loyal . . . to see you continue to succeed.'

Is It Enough?

There are four reasons battery replacements could affect I PhoneX sales:

This incident has caused significantly higher public awareness of Apple's behaviour, and thereby, the $29 offer. $29 is affordable, and it will provide a significant boost in speed (from 600MHz to 1400MHz for an iPhone 6).

Our August Wireless survey suggests battery drain is no. 1 reason for users to upgrade to new device — therefore, a new battery may deter some upgrade intention.

Apple allows for replacement regardless of the diagnostic test result. Given the same form factor from IP6 to IP8, some customers may prefer the battery swap over upgrading.

Apple's fix for this problem was to limit the peak power draw that an older iPhone was capable of through software updates.

After it revealed the fix in December, people were furious to receive confirmation from Apple that older iPhones could take longer to launch apps, may display choppy scrolling, and could have dimmer screens and quieter speakers.

Apple now has to hope that iPhone users don't decide to take a $29 battery over a $999 iPhone X.

Conclusions

1) Though Apple's strategic model cannot be said, to be distinct, they are poised on taking Amazon and Microsoft head on. Their new products, for example, iPad, suggest to be a real one in all product

for the consumers. Apple success factors suggest that they have the ability and capability to become the market leaders. The major success factor being innovation.

2) Behind their ability to innovate is its strong research and development department.

3) Its likely blockchain innovations will assist identity and information protection strategies, as we'll be far beyond using simple multifactor and even biometric protections.

4) The latest product of Apple, the iPad, however targeted on, the retired people and journalists, has received acceptance from the youth, students and the rest of the population giving Apple, a grab of the market.

Case Questions

1. How do you explain the love-hate relationship between Apple and Microsoft even though they had to mutually depend on each other even for snatched out technology from Xerox employees? Was this business or personal rivalry between Steve and Gates?

2. What was the Korean companies the Samsung doing when Apple and Microsoft were busy building their empires in US. How could they suddenly shock the market almost dethroning these behemoths?

3. Do you suspect any role Samsung has in decrying Apple on slow batteries complaint in the background of its own burnt fingers during Samsung S7 models catching fire and exploding which had almost black listed Samsung for a yearlong disaster at Market Place?

4. Why is Apple coming out clearly and boldly on to take up the issue of slowing down batteries in older models by clarifying the real reasons based on scientific investigations rather than offering battery replacement at 30% price reduction. Is Apple hiding more than its offer to come out clean?

14

The Indian Telecom Distress

A Case Study on the Severe Competition in the Telecom Sector

Learning Objectives

Rendered helpless further due to unexpected retrospective adjusted gross revenue taxes (AGR) by the government the few of the major players and their foreign partners are under severe stress not knowing the way forward to sustain business and simultaneously fight out for the enlarging telecom spectrum opportunities This is a catch 22 situation for the players in the telecom sector unless they comply with tax as demanded, they will not only loose the market share but find it difficult to survive. Several attempts to per sue the regulatory authorities to defer the AGR tax demand and legal remedies are close shut for these players. This case study tries to high light few of the issues overstressing the telecom sector which is under a duopolistic conundrum at present.

Synopsis

This case study is about stress and survival of telecom industry players. India's telecommunication network is the second largest in the world by number of telephone user (for both fixed and mobile phone). The major players are Airtel, BSNL, Vodafone-Idea. If we look back in to the history Reliance communication launched in the telecom industry in the year 2002. Later on other global measure launched in India like Vodafone, Uninor, Docomo.

Current scenario in the telecom industry—where we have disruption in the call charge prizing with lowest ever monthly rental launched by Jio

Indian Business Case Studies. V P Pawar, Bhagyashree Kunte, and Srinivas Tumuluri, Oxford University Press.
© ASM Group of Institutes, Pune, India 2022. DOI: 10.1093/oso/9780192869388.003.0014

(Mukesh Ambani group). After launch of Jio, the existing stabilize private player Airtel, Vodafone-Idea faced challenges of survival due to low AGR. This case will highlight policies that depart from telecom sector. They must reconsider or update in order to offer the best consumer experience and prizing war. This case will highlight telecom crisis. The department of telecommunication appears to be on the side of operators but survivors are still in trouble. The battle between Jio, Airtel, and Vodafone-Idea—it became very intense. Cellular Operators Association of India (COAI) came to Airtel and Vodafone Idea for support. The COAI warned Supreme Court that the telecom sector would turn into a monopoly if Jio allowed to behave on own wish without proper policies in place. However this did not go well with Jio and they shot off a letter to COAI talking about the sector. Jio said, 'these operators anyways were not investing sufficiently in the sector and have been shedding crocodile tears by claiming financial stress for a long time now and have not shown any inclination to modernize the networks.'

Case Details

Chairman Sunil Mittal called on the government to ensure that the Indian telecom market continues to have three private carriers. He also urged the centre and the judiciary to give 'sympathetic consideration' to the industry's appeal for relief after the Supreme Court's order on AGR left companies struggling.

Mittal also said the telecom regulator needs to urgently intervene to fix a floor price for tariffs. This, he said, is required for the average revenue per user (ARPU) to rise to Rs 200 initially, and to Rs 300 over time, for the industry to be healthy and sustainable.

'The situation is dire—it is a matter of survival for everyone. Vodafone (Idea) is in losses, Airtel is in losses, (state-owned) BSNL (Bharat Sanchar Nigam Ltd) is in losses,' Mittal said.

'We've been Killing Each Other.'

'There is one competitor who has unlimited access to finances—I wouldn't comment on that but the situation is bad,' he said soon after a meeting with Department of Telecommunications (DoT) Secretary Anshu Prakash on Wednesday. 'We have gone through several crises but this is the most difficult time for the industry,' Mittal added. The presence of more companies is key to consumers being well served by competition. 'It is absolutely essential that we have three (private players) plus one (state-run) players,' he said. 'Lower the taxes and find ways and means to support the sector in one form or the other.'

He urged the Supreme Court to consider Bharti's review petition with understanding.

'The honourable SC needs to look at our review petition from the point of view that there are unintended consequences and lots of other companies, including public sector, are coming into this unreasonable AGR definition, which could have never been the intention,' he said. He was referring to the government's recent clarification that the AGR order will be applicable to all telecom licensees, which includes companies such as GAIL, RailTel, Power Grid, and others. These companies, which may have minor telecom businesses, may have to pay dues based on their entire revenue with retrospective effect.

'Our legal team were perhaps not able to persuade the honorable Supreme Court on the unreasonableness of DoT's AGR interpretation but equally, I think DoT didn't realize the unintended consequences on the larger ecosystem,' said Mittal, adding that the government should have a 'sympathetic view' towards the industry.

Mittal said his comments were in the context of statements made by both Vodafone Group CEO Nick Read and Vodafone Idea Chairman Kumar Mangalam Birla, both of whom have said in the recent past that the Indian telco will have to shut if it doesn't get any relief on AGR dues. 'It will be very self-serving for me to say that two plus one is fine. I, as a person who has watched this industry from scratch—I was the first private sector guy in telecom—so, from that point of view I think India needs three plus one,' Mittal said, referring to analysts who have said that Bharti Airtel stands to gain if Vodafone-Idea collapses. He pointed out China, the world's largest market, has three and the US has four operators.

Moratorium Not Enough

The recent two-year moratorium on spectrum payments won't do much to help Vodafone Idea unless there is relief on the AGR dues. 'Otherwise, it is just deferment with interest,' Mittal said. Vodafone-Idea was left facing statutory dues of over Rs 53,000 crore, as per the telecom department's calculations, following the 24 October Supreme Court verdict that broadened the definition of AGR to include non-core items. The amount could go up, the government has said. Bharti Airtel faces over Rs 35,500 crore in additional dues comprising license fees, spectrum usage charges (SUC), interest, and penalties.

Both telcos, which have filed separate review petitions, reported record losses of over Rs 50,000 crore and Rs 23,000 crore in the July–September quarter, respectively, owing to provisions for the AGR dues. The government has previously said it can't give AGR relief, unless directed to do so by the court. License holders have to pay about 8% of AGR to DoT as fees. Telcos also need to pay 3–4% of AGR as SUC.

Fifteen telecom companies that were directly party to the case owe the government about Rs 1.47 lakh crore. The industry estimates that non-telecom companies that have telecom licences may have to pay about Rs 2.28 lakh crore, calculated from the time they got their respective permits. Mittal said that non-telecom companies such as GAIL, RailTel, Power Grid, and Delhi Metro will now be charged license fees even for the sale of gas or train tickets as per the wider interpretation of the apex court ruling, which shouldn't be the case. 'Ramifications were huge and therefore the review petition is in front of the honourable SC and we hope they will look into this whole thing,' he added.

He said the AGR dues have added to the woes of the industry, which has been swamped by 'unprecedented competition' for over three years—since the entry of Reliance Jio in September 2016—which has hurt balance sheets and caused financial stress, triggering the exit of eight operators. 'In the quest for being in the market, we have been killing each other for three and a half years,' Mittal said. 'It is an odd situation—we need a digital ecosystem to support new age industries but equally, the industry is in a crisis'.

Rare Situation

He added that setting a floor for tariffs was essential. 'It is a rare situation where we have written to the Trai (Telecom Regulatory Authority of India), saying please regulate us, because the industry is killing itself. Tariff needs to go up, industry needs to become viable,' said Mittal. 'Also, the fact that the three of us (Airtel, Reliance Jio Infocomm and Vodafone Idea) have written to the regulator says something. First time, the COAI (Cellular Operators Association of India) has an agreement to write something.' Last week, all three carriers, through COAI, asked the sector regulator to establish floor pricing for data services soon. Due to fierce rivalry, tariff correction was not possible voluntarily by any carrier, it said.

'My own view is India needs to be eventually at Rs 300 (ARPU), per month which means customers at low end need to pay about Rs 100 and higher end need to pay Rs 450–500, where they are consuming a lot,' he said. The government needs to lower levies to help the industry. 'You can't have telecom services being taxed like the sin tax! 30% of revenues are going in one form or the other—that must come down,' said Mittal.

He urged the telecom ministry to take up issues such as lowering license fees and SUC in some forum, given that the panel of secretaries set up to provide relief to the industry didn't take decisions on those matters. Mittal wasn't hopeful of a refund of the Rs 36,000 crore input tax credit lying with the finance ministry, given the government's finances.

'It is our money sitting with the government and even if they cannot refund it, can they at least offset it? Rs 36,000 crore, this is sizeable sum of money, we get no interest on this but we pay interest,' said Mittal.

He said however that Bharti Airtel was fighting it out in the marketplace. 'We are in a better situation—we have now decided to raise funds,' Mittal said. 'However, if you have to go in for network expansion, invest in newer technologies, bid for 5G spectrum and then build a 5G ecosystem which India deserves, then industry needs to be viable.'

Conclusions

Reliance Industries have invested $32bn in Jio—an entrant to India's Telecom industry, Jio attracted more than 150mn subscribers in less than 18 months. The company has transformed the Indian telecom market, mobile data consumption with its cut-rate tariffs, and triggering a wave of industry consolidation for powerful rivals, like Vodafone, Airtel, Tata, etc. This forced Anil Ambani's struggling Reliance Communications to quit the mobile sector. Reliance venture—Jio push to 'democratize the digital culture', helping vast numbers of Indians to make full use of the internet for the first time. According to rivals, Jio's success has been driven largely by unfair tactics and favourable regulatory treatment.

Jio's rivals made allegations regarding the call drop from their network, saying that the call drops resulted due to Jio's systems. This claim resonated with some analysts who noted that this was the first mobile network in the world to run entirely on 4G data technology, without any backup systems to handle voice calls.

Below points must be considered for the sector analysis:

1) Biased policies in telecom sector
2) Problem of fast-changing technology
3) Aggressive pricing forced market to port network's
4) Difficult to have a spectrum with low tariffs in the market

Thus it is important to have strong policy framework for the industry. Average revenue per connection to be increased. These two things will mainly help to avoid the financial stress on the telecom industries and consumer will have better service leading to win-win situation.

Case Questions

1. Will Government intervene to provide some relief? Discuss briefly.

2. Do you feel your use of telecommunications is supporting a competitive advantage? Can India remain with three-player market?

3. Is telecom in India becoming a duopoly?

15
Who Created the Mess?

A case study on e-mobility scenario in India

Learning Objectives

The Indian automobile industry is tied and trapped in its own mesh or mess created by sheer improvement attempts through technological advances brought in basically to edge out competitive forces and get caught into the corresponding regulatory changes calling for time-bound implementation of such technological inclusions in the basic performance criteria under regulatory essentials.

E-mobility as an alternative fuel source enabling device also comes in as a regulatory requirement compelling the entire auto sector to align for implementation of e-mobility technology in its vehicle designs as an essential step towards pollution control measure.

Synopsis

Electrical power vehicles are the new alternative to the traditional fuel like petrol, diesel, etc. Most of the major cities in India are facing a problem of pollution due to emissions from vehicles. Specifically the metros like Delhi, Bangalore are already has recorded the highest polluted city. The demands of automobile vehicles are growing day by day. There are many reasons for it. The household income per capita is increased, intense competition ended with economic selling pricing, small segment budgeted luxury cars are available, etc. It gives boost to the automobile industry. This sector contributes largely to India's GDP and also in terms of employment generation.

Indian Business Case Studies. V P Pawar, Bhagyashree Kunte, and Srinivas Tumuluri, Oxford University Press.
© ASM Group of Institutes, Pune, India 2022. DOI: 10.1093/oso/9780192869388.003.0015

Government of India recently declares that it will be mandatory for automobile industry to manufacture electric vehicle. They are targeting to be 100% electrical vehicle in 2030. They are taking steps accordingly. It will be an alarm for all automobile manufacturers to become electrical savvy. In India, there is only Mahindra and Mahindra selling the e-vehicle, i.e., Reva. The sale does not show sizable growth in recent past. Customer's preferences are not for Reva as compared to other vehicles. There are limitations like speed, weight, etc. The facts are that there is not much research had been carried out in this area. The development and technological advancement done in traditional mode of vehicles. Everyone knows that traditional source of fuel will not be long lasting but they are ignoring this fact.

The entire automobile sectors are started working on this area. Some are not be been technological savvy they are looking for tie-up with other company. Mahindra and Mahindra had a discussion of tie-up with Ford motor. Tata motor goes one step ahead to introduce 'Tigor' in electrical mode. The first batches of 10,000 vehicles are already procured. Xiaomi the cell phone manufacturing company already in the automobile electrical vehicle business in China wanted to enter in Indian market. We can say that they are veterans in this field. The traditional automobile manufacturing companies are way behind them. It's a threat to the existing automobile players.

The structure of traditional vehicles will likely to be changed drastically due to electrification. The car which manufactures by using 10,000 parts which likely to be replaced with less than 1,000 parts. It has a big impact on the overall auto ancillary industries. The existing auto ancillary industries likely to suffer. As many parts will not be required in future. These companies will be closed down in future. It directly affects on employment. Due to the requirement of reduced weight of the vehicle, company are looking for a substitute in existing raw material. It will bring down the traditional raw material requirement. In future we may find the new players will dominate this field.

The requirement of crude oil will drastically go down in this scenario. It is an alarm for crude supplying nation. They will definitely lose business that's sure. They have to come out with different thought process to sell their product.

This case is focusing on the emerging requirement with respect to electrical vehicles, automobile company's strategy to cope up with it, role of government, impact on auto ancillary sectors, impact on employment, customer expectations, requirement of research in this segment, future demand of the vehicles, substitute like gas, solar energy, etc.

Indian Automobile Industry

Indian automobile industry contributing the major percentage in country's GDP. All automobile segments like two-wheeler, four-wheeler, commercial vehicle, passenger-carrying vehicle are in the world top ten in recent past. Most of the big industries are having their presence in India. India is becoming the automobile hub.

Mahindra Takes Control of Reva Cars

Reva was founded by Maini Group by investing more than $50 million. The main aim is to develop electric vehicles. It was not easy due to high price and inappropriate infrastructures like charging stations and other facilities. Company found it difficult to run as sale was not as per expectations.

In the year 2010, Mahindra and Mahindra Ltd (M&M), India's biggest automaker takes over the stake in Reva Electric Car Co., a Bangalore based company. These moves will definitely give an edge to cope up with electric vehicle market. It will expect to grow in coming period. As strict emission norms are adopted globally. Maini continued the operations at Mahindra Reva and Mr Goenka becomes the chairman of the board. Maini families are holding about 31%, other 11%, and employees 3% are in the form of stock options.

The company buy out the promoters' stake and make Rs 45 crore as a fresh equity. In this transaction company will get a 55.2% stake. Company renamed as Mahindra Reva Electric Vehicle Co. Ltd. As per the analyst the estimated price for M&M's stake is approximately Rs 330 crore. It is based on the value of assumption that Reva's enterprise value is approximately Rs 500 crore. It is a part of strategy of Chairman Anand Mahindra for expansion of business. The company is expecting that electric and hybrid fuel technology will get an edge in coming years. Company does that not for the 'investment point of view' but they want to increase their capability by having an advantage over competitors. Mahindra & Mahindra also acquires the Satyam Computer Services Ltd and Kinetic Motor Company in 2008.

Mr Pawan Goenka of M&M said he did not expect to see profits right away and declined to say when he expected Mahindra Reva to break even. He is expected to sell 50,000 units a year in coming next seven to eight years. They are estimating the global electric vehicle market will definitely grow in 2020. General Motor (GM) was a strategic partner for Reva. Earlier Reva cars were sold only through showrooms of Delhi and Bangalore. The sale begins with the 70–75 dealers of M&M. It also sells in 24 different countries in Europe, Asia, Chile, South Africa, and Brazil. In the year 2012, Mahindra Reva, the electric car manufacturer targets to sell 30,000 units of battery-operated cars in the year by 2015–2016. Their production capacity is to manufacture 6,000 from its Bangalore plant. M&M comes out with new car called e20. In 2016, they got orders of 1250 units from other country.

M&M have already launched the electric three-wheeler, i.e., Bijlee in the year 1999 and sold more than 50,000 vehicles of their popular model Scorpio in micro-hybrid type. Reva has sold 3,500 cars since 2001. It was launched in two-door passenger car category.

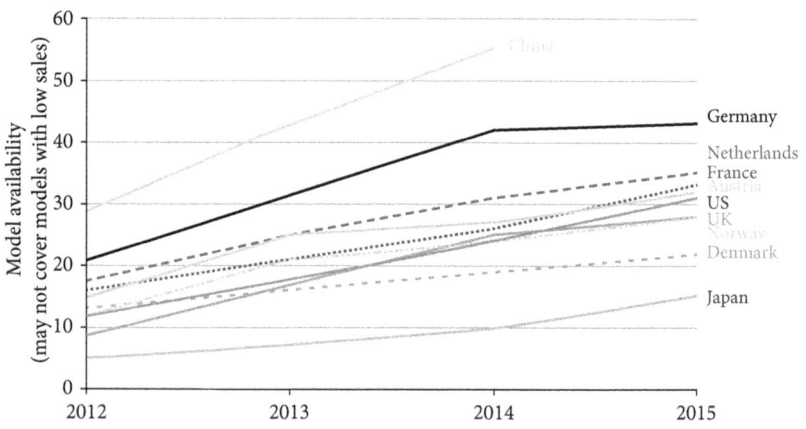

India's Anticipated Growth of Electric Vehicle in 2022

The government aiming to electrify all vehicles in country by 2032.

Government declares that they will prefer the electric vehicle in future. That may be the end of traditional fuel consumption vehicles. They are recommended the lower taxation and interest rates for loans on electric vehicles. They are also thinking to open up the battery plant by 2018 and charging stations for electric vehicles. Electric vehicles gaining importance in current policy by getting incentive and research funding for both hybrid vehicles (which combine fossil fuel and electric power) and electric cars.

In fact the incentives are as high as Rs 1,40,000 on few selected cars; the scheme has made only a little progress. The sales of electric and hybrid cars making up only a fraction of the 3 million (30 lakh) passenger vehicles sold in India in 2016.

There Are Lot of Development Was Done in the Year 2017

1. There are 200 charging stations are proposed in Chandigarh, Delhi, and Jaipur.
2. Delhi government already declares the subsidy of Rs 30,000/- for e-rickshaw in 2016. This segment expected to rise by 50% in 2022.
3. Government targeting around 6 million electric and hybrid vehicles on road by 2020.
4. Companies are also announced investment of Rs 1000 crores charging infrastructure.

Response from Automobile Sector

Maruti Suzuki has invested in mild-hybrid technology, which makes lesser use of electric power than full hybrids.

Toyota Motor Corp sells its ultra-luxury sedan of hybrid Camry in the country.

Mahindra & Mahindra is the only manufacturer of electric vehicles in India.

Cummins India, the engine maker has invested in research on electric mobility solutions for India. Hyundai Motor Co has started looking components for electric cars. They had started discussing with its supplier.

Ashok Leyland launched an electric bus in the year 2015–2016. They are partnered with Indian start-up SUN Mobility. They start developing battery-swapping technology for buses, cars, and trucks.

Electrification of mobility products segment opens up new opportunities for new players. The existing players would need to develop, adapt, and adjust with change. India's technology requirements for electric vehicles are different from that of the West due to the unique and different environmental conditions, driving pattern, road condition, geographical location, climate. Investment in electric technology and build up infrastructure for charging has huge potential and definite return on investment. OEM is looking for development and production of ICE (Internal Combustion Engine) for vehicle but electrification requires the alternative. It definitely gives the birth of electrification era. The replacement of a BS-VI (Gasoline or Diesel Engine) with an electric motor. At great extent it reduces the complexity in engineering. This change is inevitable. A company has to come out with new strategies.

Fact Lies in Electrification

Most of India's and MNC's automakers are criticized government to move for full electrification of India's vehicles by 2030. Mercedes Benz India's Roland Folger has stated that unless India moves away from electricity produced from coal, to non-polluting sources of electricity, electric cars will be more polluting than Bharat Stage 6 emission norms compliant petrol and diesel cars. Toyota India's top management is also said that hybrid cars are to be encouraged as a bridge before complete electrification of cars. Charging of cars like e2oPlus at home or regular charging using a regular 15amp charging socket. The process takes 8–9 hours with a standard charge and in fast charging it takes 1.5 hours. It can cover distance around 140km on a full charging. It is restricted due to limited charging network and long charging time.

Electric load shedding is a major problem as the electricity supply outside of most tier-I cities is inconsistent. The impact of batteries on environment if not properly recycled. Batteries are working by converting the chemical energy into electrical energy. Chemicals inside the battery are cadmium, lead, mercury, nickel, lithium, and electrolytes. If these chemicals are burned underground for a long period of time, it is harmful for human.

Company Strategies

The structure of traditional vehicles will likely be changed drastically due to electrification. The car which manufactures by using 10,000 parts which likely to be replaced with less than 1,000 parts. It has a big impact on the overall auto ancillary industries. The existing auto ancillary industries likely to suffer. As many parts will not be required in future. These companies will be closed down in future. It directly affects on employment. Due to the requirement of reduced weight of the vehicle, company are looking for substitute in existing raw material. It will bring down the traditional raw material requirement. In future we may find the new players will dominate this field.

The requirement of crude oil will drastically go down in this scenario. It is an alarm for crude supplying nation. They will definitely lose business that's sure. They have to come out with different thought process to sell their product. The problems of pollution due to battery problems will arise.

This case is focusing on the emerging requirement with respect to electrical vehicles, automobile company's strategy to cope up with it, role of government, impact on auto ancillary sectors, impact on employment, customer expectations, requirement of research in this segment, future demand of the vehicles, substitute like gas, solar energy, etc.

Case Questions

1. Suggest the appropriate strategies for automobile companies to sustain in this scenario.

2. Suggest the alternate fuel source for automobile sectors with justification.

3. Do you agree with government announcement of electrification in automobile sector?

16

Coca-Cola: 'Taste the Controversy'

A Case Study on Marketing Challenges

Learning Objectives

To study marketing challenges posed by changing environment. To study the importance of corporate and product image in marketing of the product. To study the importance of customer perception of the product and the company and company ethics. To study the role of marketing communication in creating positive image of the product.

Synopsis

The not so lucky situations and criticism of the Coca-Cola brand come from its first-ever product. As the history from many sources says, Dr John Smith-Pemberton, Coca-Cola creator, fought in the Civil War, and had some injuries. He made a special formula in order to help him deal with the constant pain in his body: the Pemberton's French Wine Coca which also had a great taste at the time, had alcohol in it. It quickly became very popular until a vote by the state legislature Atlanta and Fulton County in favour of the national temperance movement.

The national temperance movement prohibited the use of alcohol and heavily criticized medicinal wine such as French Wine Coca. Pemberton was forced to drop the wine ingredient in his French Wine Coca. After some further experimenting, he decided on the use of sugar syrup as a substitution for the wine and that is when Coca-Cola was born. He invented many drugs, but none of them ever made any money. So, after a move to Atlanta, Pemberton decided to try his hand in the beverage market. In his time, the soda fountain was rising in popularity as a social gathering spot.

Indian Business Case Studies. V P Pawar, Bhagyashree Kunte, and Srinivas Tumuluri, Oxford University Press.
© ASM Group of Institutes, Pune, India 2022. DOI: 10.1093/oso/9780192869388.003.0016

Temperance was keeping patrons out of bars, so making a soda-fountain drink just made sense. And this was when Coca-Cola was born.

However, Pemberton had no idea how to advertise. This is where Frank Robinson came in. He registered Coca-Cola's formula with the patent office, and he designed the logo. He also wrote the slogan, 'The Pause That Refreshes'. Coke did not do so well in its first year. And to make matters worse, Doc Pemberton (who invented the formula in 1886) died in August 1888, meaning he would never see the commercial success he had been seeking.

After Pemberton's death, a man named Asa Griggs Candler rescued the business. In 1891, he became the sole owner of Coca-Cola. A controversial move on the part of Candler was to sell Coca-Cola syrup as a patent medicine, claiming it would get rid of fatigue and headaches.

In 1898, however, Congress passed a tax in the wake of the Spanish-American war. The tax was on all medicines, so Coca-Cola wanted to be sold only as a beverage. After a court battle, Coca-Cola was no longer sold as a drug.

Now, the Coca-Cola Company is one the most renowned beverage companies in the world. It owns the majority of the soft drink market around the world, distributing roughly 160 different products. According to Forbes Magazine, Coca-Cola is one of the world's most innovative companies with a net worth of 192.8 billion. Since the early 2000s, the criticisms over the use of Coca-Cola products as well as the company itself, escalated with concerns over health effects, environmental issues, animal testing, economic business practices, and employee issues. The Coca-Cola Company has been faced with multiple lawsuits concerning the various criticisms, fuelled by social media, especially in the last few years.

Rumours, Myths, and Truth

According to Coca-Cola, Pemberton brewed the first mix of his new drink in his backyard, using a modest three-legged kettle. Coca-Cola also states that cocaine was never an ingredient in the elixir.

According to Mark Pendergrast, author of 'For God, Country & Coca-Cola', the syrup was meant to go along with the culture of the times. The syrup was to be advertised as a 'nerve tonic' to calm people down. Also, it was advertised under Candler's reign to cure headaches and fatigue. Pendergrast also says that Coca-Cola did in fact have a negligible amount of cocaine in it. Even though Candler said he would shut down the Coca-Cola operation if the drink was found to be harmful, the drink did contain coca leaves.

The syrup had one half-ounce of coca leaf per gallon, amounting to about a little over one-hundredth of a grain. Coca-Cola was named for its two principal drug ingredients. Coca leaf from Peru contained cocaine. Kola nut from Ghana contained caffeine. Original Coca-Cola had a very small amount of cocaine in a six-ounce drink, about 4.3 milligrams. The company took out all but a minuscule amount of cocaine in 1903 and the final amount in 1928. It made the drink very controversial, but it also contributed to Coca-Cola's success.

Coca-Cola is not fascinating for what it is—coloured sugar water with bubbles—but for what it represents. And that's a point long known by the company's marketers, with the exception of when they forgot it during the New Coke fiasco in the 1980s. Today, marketing students in business schools everywhere study that famous gaff.

Despite the decades-old slogan, 'Delicious and Refreshing', people do not drink Coca-Cola for the taste. They drink it because they associate it with positive things like friendship, fun, patriotism, and athleticism. Careful to market the drink to all people, everywhere, without alienating anyone, the ads are often vague. 'Coke is It!' What is 'it'? It's whatever you want it to be, just as long as it makes you want to buy more Coke!

Ethical Waters

The company claims to adhere to the 'highest ethical standards' and to be 'an outstanding corporate citizen in every community we serve'. Yet Coca-Cola's activities around the world tell a different story.

Many documentaries have surfaced with strong accusations, from helping spreading obesity, race discrimination, causing extreme water shortages in developing countries where supplies are scarce and killing union leaders around the globe. Some websites are dedicated to persuade the consumers and informing them about alleged cases of corruption, support of military groups, and many other issues that are becoming more evident every day. The evidence of surpassing the law in the third world and developing countries is growing and users in social media are listening and sharing, not worrying about all of this is true or false. New evidence from campaign group War on Want appears to show that Coca-Cola has had a serious impact in communities in several countries. Colombia, Guatemala, Turkey, China, Mexico, Salvador, India, and the list could go on.

In 2006, for example, War on Want researchers have uncovered areas in Rajasthan, India, where farmers have been unable to irrigate their fields after Coca-Cola established a bottling plant. The War on Want report also revealed similar problems in Uttar Pradesh. Already well-known are incidents in the southern Indian state of Kerala, where a Coke plant was forced to close two years ago after it was alleged to have contaminated local water.

Coca-Cola is the largest beverage company in the world, and used 283 billion litres of water in 2004. For every 2.7 litres of water it takes, it produces one litre of product. Its profits last year were just under $15bn and it has a market capitalization of over $100bn. But the firm faces a string of environmental and health issues. It has also endured some embarrassing PR disasters, as when it was forced to withdraw a premium brand of bottled water from the UK after it emerged that it was processed tap water.

Louis Richards added: 'Across the world, cases of environmental damage, exploitation of water resources and abuses of workers' rights are shockingly common. It's time that directors of multinationals held to account—but that will only happen when politicians accept that the current free-for-all is failing the world's poor.'

The attacks came as critics rounded on Coca-Cola for sponsoring the World Water Forum, currently taking place in Mexico. The forum is a place where water firms, technicians, environmentalists, and consultants discuss how to improve conditions for the 1.1 billion people who do not have access to safe water and sanitation, but it has come under attack for being a talking shop that achieves little.

A Coca-Cola spokesman said: 'We have a genuine commitment to adequate and equitable access to water. We have reduced our water-use ratios in India by 24 per cent between 2000 and 2004. We have installed rainwater harvesting systems in 26 of our plants so far.' Coca-Cola's own workers have also suffered and the company is being increasingly associated with anti-union activities. The most notable case is in Colombia, where paramilitaries have killed eight Coca-Cola workers since 1990. The main Coca-Cola trade union Sinaltrainal is seeking to hold Coca-Cola liable for using paramilitaries to engage in anti-union violence.

Coca-Cola is being sued on behalf of transport workers and their families for its part in the alleged intimidation and torture of trade unionists and their families by special branch police in Turkey. In Nicaragua, workers of the main Coca-Cola union SUTEC have been denied the right to organize and the General Secretary of SUTEC, Daniel Reyes, believes the objective of this ongoing and escalating campaign is to crush the union.

Guatemalan workers have been struggling against Coca-Cola since the 1970s. In the years between 1976 and 1985, three general secretaries of the main union were assassinated and members of their families, friends, and legal advisers were threatened, arrested, kidnapped, shot, tortured, and forced into exile. The violations of workers' rights continue. And Coca-Cola workers and their family members, with ties to unions, have reportedly been subjected to death threats. Elsewhere in countries such as Peru, Russia, and Chile, Coca-Cola workers have been protesting against the company's anti-union policies. Coca-Cola claims to exist 'to benefit and refresh everyone it touches' and to try to sustain this positive image, the company spends $2 billion a year on advertising alone. Yet there are signs that the image is beginning to crumble. The relay carrying the Olympic flame was repeatedly disrupted by protests at Coca-Cola's role as the principal sponsor, with the Turin council actually declaring the city a no-go zone for the company (a decision subsequently overruled by the mayor).

University campuses throughout the USA and Europe have voted to cancel contracts with Coca-Cola in protest at its operations, and in solidarity with the community resistance which has escalated in many countries across the world. It is up to us to keep up the pressure on Coca-Cola and also send a strong message to our elected leaders to rein in irresponsible business practices.

Drinking Obesity?

According to the Centers for Disease Control and Prevention (CDC), around half of the US population drink sugary beverages on any given day, with consumption of these drinks highest among teenagers and young adults. There are approximately 10 teaspoons of added sugar in a single can of cola. The World Health Organization (WHO) recommend consuming no more than six teaspoons of added sugar daily, meaning drinking just one serving of cola a day could take us well above these guidelines.

As such, it is no surprise that sugary drink consumption is associated with an array of health conditions. According to the Harvard School of Public Health, people who drink 1–2 cans of sugary beverages daily are 26% more likely to develop type 2 diabetes, and last month, Medical News Today reported on a study claiming 184,000 global deaths each year are down to sugary drink consumption.

Now, an info graphic created by British pharmacist Niraj Naik—based on research by health writer Wade Meredith—shows the damage a 330 ml can of Coca-Cola can do to the body within 1 hour of consumption. Coca-Cola is 'comparable to heroin' in how it stimulates the brain's reward and pleasure centres.

According to Naik, the intense sweetness of Coca-Cola as a result of its high sugar content should make us vomit as soon as it enters the body. However, the phosphoric acid in the beverage dulls the sweetness, enabling us to keep the drink down.

Blood sugar levels increase dramatically within 20 minutes of drinking the Cola, explains Naik, causing a burst of insulin. The liver then turns the high amounts of sugar circulating our body into fat.

Within 40 minutes, the body has absorbed all of the caffeine from the Cola, causing a dilation of pupils and an increase in blood pressure. By this point, the adenosine receptors in the brain have been blocked, preventing fatigue.

Five minutes later, production of dopamine has increased—a neurotransmitter that helps control the pleasure and reward centres of the brain. According to the info graphic, the way Coca-Cola stimulates these centres is comparable to the effects of heroin, making us want another can.

An hour after drinking the beverage, a sugar crash will begin, causing irritability and drowsiness. In addition, the water from the Cola will have been cleared from the body via urination, along with nutrients that are important for our health.

According to Naik, the info graphic is not only applicable to Coca-Cola, but to all caffeinated fizzy drinks.

'Coke is not just high in high fructose corn syrup, but it is also packed with refined salts and caffeine,' writes Naik on his blog 'The Renegade Pharmacist'. 'Regular consumption of these ingredients in the high quantities you find in Coke and other processed foods and drinks, can lead to higher blood pressure, heart disease, diabetes and obesity.'

'However a small amount now and then won't do any major harm,' he adds. 'The key is moderation.'

In a press statement, a spokesperson for Coca-Cola says the beverage is 'perfectly safe to drink and can be enjoyed as part of a balanced diet and lifestyle.'

Coca-Cola responded to *The New York Times* article with a statement from Dr Ed Hays, the company's chief technical officer. He describes the article as an inaccurate portrayal of the company by claiming Coca-Cola was funding research to convince people that diets don't matter, only exercise.

'At Coke, we believe that a balanced diet and regular exercise are two key ingredients for a healthy lifestyle and that is reflected in both our long-term and short-term business actions,' he states.

This response distances the company from the overt and problematic claims made by one of GEBN's executives. However, it is the mere presence of Coca-Cola as a major funding source for the organization that is an issue for some public health experts.

Industry funding of research is commonplace and, unfortunately, studies have demonstrated that funding sources can influence the outcomes of clinical trials.

A systematic review of 206 studies and reviews about soft drinks, juice, and milk was conducted and published in PLOS Medicine in 2007. Of these articles, 111 declared financial sponsorship, with 22% receiving industry funding, 47% receiving no industry funding, and 32% receiving mixed funding.

A hand holding a glass of cola.

Multiple studies indicate that industry funding increases the likelihood of a study producing positive results. Among interventional studies, the researchers found that 0% of the studies with any industry funding came to unfavourable conclusions compared with 37% of the studies with no industry funding. The authors stated their study indicated that beverage industry-funded studies are four to eight times more likely to produce results favourable to the industry in comparison with studies that are independently funded.

A similar level of bias has been found in other studies examining the influence of pharmaceutical company funding on drug trials and for-profit organizations on trials of new treatment strategies. The findings of such studies suggest that the financial support Coca-Cola gives to GEBN could be very influential in the researchers' output. The article in *The New York Times* states that the company donated $1.5 million last year to set up the organization, while nearly $4 million in funding has been provided since 2008 to Dr Blair and another GEBN executive, Gregory A. Hand.

Even if the research conducted can be proved to be influenced by bias, however, experts believe that the mere existence of such research contributes to 'health halo legitimization'. Marion Nestle, a professor of nutrition, food studies and public health at New York University, says that the agenda is to 'get these researchers to confuse the science and deflect attention from dietary intake'.

Creating Doubt: Comparisons with Big Tobacco

Dr Bruce Lee, director of the Global Obesity Prevention Center at Johns Hopkins University, told Health line that Coca-Cola and GEBN's arrangement crosses a line by promoting a view that sits outside of scientific consensus. 'When you start trying to say that something is a greater cause of obesity, that's potentially when we get into a problem,' he said.

The article in *The New York Times* compares what Coca-Cola is doing with GEBN with a well-documented strategy employed by tobacco companies: paying for health experts to create doubt about the health hazards of smoking. Last month, *Medical News Today* reported on a study that analysed cases in which patients were suing tobacco companies for damages.

The researchers discovered that a group of physicians testified for the tobacco industry against patients dying of cancer on multiple occasions, repeatedly stating that their smoking did not cause cancer. Three major tobacco companies—R.J. Reynolds, Philip Morris, and Lorillard—paid a pool of six board-certified otolaryngologists to testify in over 50 cases, using methods to support their testimony that researchers deemed unscientific.

'By highlighting an exhaustive list of potential risk factors, such as alcohol, diesel fumes, machinery fluid, salted fish, reflux of stomach acid, mouthwash and even urban living, they created doubt in the minds of the jurors as to the role of smoking in the plaintiff's cancer,' the authors report. With the prevalence of obesity and sugary drinks in the US, arrangements such as the one between Coca-Cola and GEBN cannot but appear problematic. The CDC state that around half of the US population consume sugary beverages every day.

While many policy-making groups are looking to reduce the rate at which such beverages are consumed, the existence of scientific research arguing that sugary drinks are not hazardous to health will prove to be a stumbling block.

Consuming small amounts of sugary drinks from time to time will not necessarily harm an individual, but repeated messages suggesting that such drinks are fine and that exercise is more important could have a long-lasting effect on public health.

The End of the Coke Era?

Lara O'Reilly in Business Insider Website wrote down an article about this phenomenon.

Too many times in recent months, headline writers have had reason to write that 'Coke is losing its fizz'.

Pepsi-Cola surpassed Diet Coke to become the second-biggest soda brand in the US, Coca-Cola's biggest market, Beverage Digest reported last month. Diet Coke had been the second-biggest soda brand by volume in the US since 2010, but Pepsi's shift back to No. 2 provided evidence of America's growing dislike for diet sodas—and that is at a time when Americans are drinking less soda overall than in the 1980s.

Before that report was published, Coca-Cola reported that net earnings attributable to shareholders plunged 55% in its fourth quarter to $770 million. Net operating revenue dropped 2% in the quarter to $10.9 billion (but global sales did increase slightly over the full year). North America, its biggest market, saw a modest sales rise for the first time in four quarters.

The long-term picture is worse. In 2014, global revenue was $46 billion, down 4% ($2 billion less) from 2012. This downward trajectory isn't due to a sudden, major catalyst. As Beverage Digest's report explains (emphasis added): 'Brand Coke's volume was up (0.1%), but just barely. However, the brand was up, after multiple years of decline. The last time brand Coke grew was 2000.'

Globally, Coca-Cola has been missing its own 3% to 4% annual volume growth target for two years, as this chart—drawn from data compiled by *The Wall Street Journal*—indicates.

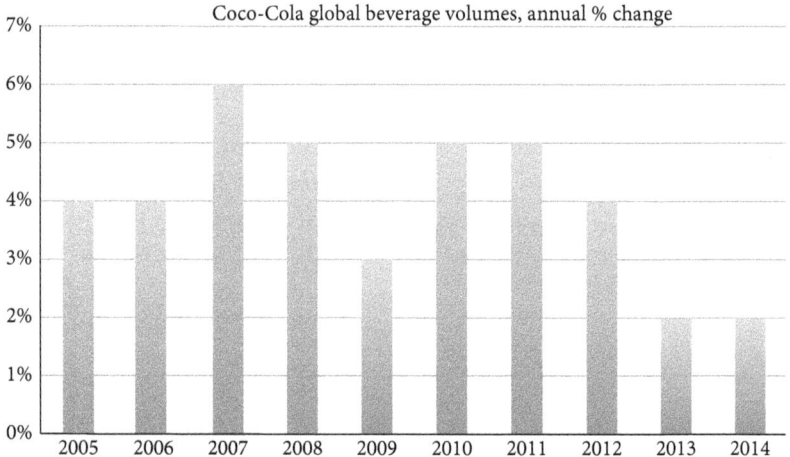

Coco-Cola global beverage volumes, annual % change

Coca-Cola/The Wall Street Journal/Business Insider

It's not just Coke experiencing this issue, the entire soda market in the US, picking out one region as an example, is in decline. The attention is on Coke because it is the leader of the sector. It may yet be decades before people start referring to Coke in the same way they do Kodak, and its terminal decline may not even happen at all. But if the company does not make a big strategic move soon, a massively mature market could be coming to an end. Right now, Coke is on the way out. Not with a bang, but a long, slow whimper.

Coca-Cola's CEO Muhtar Kent said 2015 would be a 'transition year', and that it would like time for the benefits of the $3 billion cost-cutting plan it announced in October to materialize 'amidst an uncertain and volatile macroeconomic environment'.

The 'transition' Kent is looking for is already evident in some of its most recent actions: It has invited 10 agencies to pitch ideas for its next global marketing campaign. In Europe it has redesigned the packaging across all its different flavours to look the same, and it is dropping its marketing for individual brands like Diet Coke and Coke Zero. All marketing will instead be consolidated under the Coca-Cola brand in the region (you will still see other products from the portfolio in ads, but there will be no more individual ads like the famous 'Diet Coke hunk' campaign).

But as sales continue to fall from previous heights as consumers change their drinking habits, opting for healthier beverages (its portfolio of sugary drinks is another reason Coke often hits the headlines for negative reasons) are the big marketing changes coming all too late, or can they really save the company from falling into a terminal decline?

'The Days of Coke Being the World's Biggest Brand Are over Forever'

No matter which stat you look at, Coke's value as a business appears to be eroding.

In recent years, Coca-Cola has been edged out of the top five in BrandZ's annual 'top 100 most valuable brands' rankings by tech companies, and even McDonald's. Coca-Cola does fare better in Interbrand's annual rankings—coming third last year, behind Google (2) and Apple (1). But Coke is unlikely to dominate those lists again, according to Melbourne Business School associate professor of marketing, branding consultant, and Marketing Week columnist Mark Ritson.

He told Business Insider: 'Coke will always be the leading brand of cola until the end of time. But the value of that cola category is set to plummet over the next 20 years. It's no good being a big fish in an ever smaller pond. The days of Coke being the world's biggest brand are over forever.'

And that's down to nuanced drinking habits becoming more widespread, Ritson added: 'Natural products, organic ingredients, incredibly fresh origin, local provenance—these were initially the watchwords of small groups of maven consumers, but this movement has become more and more pronounced in the developed world in recent years. And it will only get stronger in the years to come. The very success and former dominance of Coca-Cola during the 20th century blinded them to the very different market conditions that the 21st century ushered in and left them suddenly vulnerable to change.'

The Move to Master the Brand

Coke's move across Europe to advertise its entire range, rather than each brand separately, has some clear advantages: It eases confusion around its ever-increasing portfolio of brand extensions; it shifts focus away from its unhealthier products to low or no calorie variants; and it has the potential to cut costs.

Coca-Cola tells us that the move is not about cutting marketing investment (on the contrary, it plans to increase investment in the Coca-Cola trademark in Great Britain, for example), but there will no doubt be savings in areas where there are now crossovers.

We asked what would happen to the brand managers and marketing managers who worked on specific brands like Diet Coke or Coke Zero. A Coca-Cola spokeswoman told us that the company is going through a global reorganization that will affect 1,600 to 1,800 roles across corporate, Coca-Cola North America, and Coca-Cola International—but it's too soon to say how many roles will be impacted in Europe.

The move to the master brand approach could well be adopted in North America and other global markets too. The result of its recent ad agency pitch will likely see the end of the brand's six-year 'Open Happiness' activity and a push into a new creative direction for the flagship red Coca-Cola brand.

In a statement the company said: 'We have invited a selection of our key agencies from around the world to bring their best thinking to Coca-Cola in order to create the strongest work for our flagship brand. We are always pushing ourselves and our agencies to deliver world class creative with global appeal that engages and entertains our consumers and drives business growth. This process will help us harness thinking from some of the best agency minds from around the world to deliver the best possible work.'

Elspeth Cheung, global BrandZ valuation director, told Business Insider that Coca-Cola's recent campaign to celebrate the 100th anniversary of its famous contoured bottle, setting up retro-themed pop-up shops in major cities, and a wider advertising push 'starring' icons like Elvis Presley and Marilyn Monroe shows the power of the master brand still exists today.

Cheung said: 'There are few other brands that could challenge Coke by matching this, and this is all due to the historical cultivation of the Coca-Cola master brand. If anything is going to revive the business, it will be this signature brand—which is the most recognized around the world.'

However, Cheung adds: 'I would advise the brand owner not to concentrate on the cost saving advantage that the use of master brand will bring about. BrandZ research shows that brands in categories such as beer and cars which have shifted the focus to the operational advantages of global economies of scale have caused their brands to become less unique and distinctive.'

Jamal Benmiloud, a former vice president of marketing at Monster Energy (and former UK head of marketing at Red Bull), who is now the chief creative officer and founder of marketing agency EARN, thinks Coke has the power to change opinion not just by the way it communicates, but a different business approach.

'I think they have the opportunity to be true to their values and do more in terms of giving back. It may create a negative reaction, but so what, it's about doing the right thing. Coca-Cola should be the most entertaining, anticipated brand in the world, and they should also be loved in the same way someone like Princess Diana was loved by committing to causes and making the difference. They have the power to do amazing things on planet earth,' Benmiloud said.

A great example of this is Coke's project in partnership with other charities to lend its vast distribution and logistics network to help deliver essential medicines to remote African villages. 'You need to give to get love, and we need to see more giving of love,' Benmiloud, who co-authored the recently published book 'Brand Love: How to Build a Brand Worth Talking About', added, saying Coke has the ability to fund more such initiatives.

One of the things that has characterized Muhtar Kent's reign at the top of Coca-Cola is his long-term outlook for the company. In 2010 he outlined the company's '2020 Vision', built around six socio-economic trends that it hopes will help it double revenue by 2020. Other strategies are also given long-term completion dates, like its ambition to get 1 million people more physically active in Great Britain by 2020.

Benmiloud comments: 'One thing about Coke that really impresses me is how long in the game they are, they really think long-term. They may be having a difficult time right now, but it has a plan for five, 15, 20 years on how to grow as a company ... I think Coke's at a certain point in its history and we'll see what it does in the next five years, and what it does to embrace people and its partners to get there.'

Diversification will also be key if Coke is to adapt to ever-changing consumer consumption trends, and the company is already making inroads in that area. Earlier this year it launched a premium milk called Fair life in the US, for example, and last year Coca-Cola paid $2.15 billion for a 16.7% stake in Monster Energy to help expand its reach in the energy drinks market. And in 2013 Coke increased its stake in Innocent Drinks to almost 100% in a bid to grow its share of the European smoothie and juices market.

But Coke still has work to do, according to Ritson: 'PepsiCo is in a much stronger position versus Coca-Cola because it derives less than half its global profits from soda beverages, compared to 75% of revenues at Coca-Cola. That screams out an obvious and urgent fix. Coca-Cola needs to maintain Coke sales as much as possible and manage the decline as well as they can while urgently looking to diversify and acquire new brands that are fit for the 21st century.'

The Coke era as we know it is probably over. But a new, more diverse era for Coke is just beginning.

Case Questions

1. Do you think Coca-Cola will surpass the scandals around the world like it did in the past?

2. Do some extra research; do you think all the news and rumours are true?

3. What do you think about Coca-Cola's ethics?

4. Do you think social media is a key factor for the Coca-Cola sales sinking?

5. What do you think about Coca-Cola 2020 strategy? Do you think it will be enough to rescue the brand from the low sales?

6. What's your opinion about Pepsi scaling position when Coca-Cola is losing market share?

7. Do you think the megatrend on health concerns will affect Pepsi and Coca-Cola in a long term?

8. Suggest a product and marketing communication strategy for improving the image of the company and its products.

17

Holding On and Letting It Go

A Case Study on Issues at Infosys India

Learning Objectives

To understand the importance of corporate culture of an organization. To understand effect of corporate culture on the working of organization and expectations from employees.

Case details

Mr Salil Parekh the new CEO of Infosys joined with a warm welcome reception from the Infosys employees seated in the plush CEO office of the headquarters and was preparing mentally for the board meeting to be held at 12 noon. Mr Salil Parekh had taken over as a CEO from Mr U B Pravin Rao who acted as the interim CEO of the company. The interim period was from 18 August 2017 to 1 January 2018 wherein Mr Rao was brought in as the Interim CEO after the conflict between Mr Vishal Sikka who resigned as CEO from 18 August 2017 and Mr Narayana Murthy the Iconic Co-Founder. The new CEO, Mr Parekh is not really new to Infosys. In fact, he was in the race for the post of CEO along with Mr Vishal Sikka in the year 2014, wherein Mr Sikka won the race and became the CEO of Infosys. Subsequent to the turn of events and conflict between Mr Narayana Murthy and Mr Vishal Sikka led to the resignation of Mr Sikka. Consequently, the hunt for new CEO began and this time Mr Parekh became the winner with the annual salary of variable Rs 9.75 crore and fixed Rs 6.5 crore with a total of Rs 16.25 crore.

Indian Business Case Studies. V P Pawar, Bhagyashree Kunte, and Srinivas Tumuluri, Oxford University Press.
© ASM Group of Institutes, Pune, India 2022. DOI: 10.1093/oso/9780192869388.003.0017

Infosys India's Most Admired Company

In January 1981, Mr Narayana Murthy and six engineers met in a tiny rented apartment in Pune, in western India, to develop the vision for a new company, Infosys Technology Ltd, that would provide software development and maintenance services for the domestic and export markets. The company started with an initial capital of $250 that Murthy borrowed by pawning his wife's jewellery. The founders transformed the company to a NASDAQ' Listed as Global IT services and consulting firm with annual revenue of seven billion dollars and an employee base of more than 1,50,000 professional, across 68 offices and 70 development centres worldwide. Throughout the history of the company, founders had held the post of CEO and managing director that, Mr Shibbulal would be the last founding CEO to lead the company.

Mr Vishal Sikka Became the CEO

Mr Vishal Sikka joined Infosys Ltd. on 12 June 2014, after the then CEO Mr Shibbulal left, to help transform the company during a time of significant change in the service industry. The significant change was brought on by the cost imperatives of the client on one hand, significant and rapid advancements in technology on the other hand. Since joining Infosys, Mr Sikka has implemented a strategy of helping clients renew their existing landscapes to fundamentally drive down cost using automation and artificial intelligence, and at the same time brings breakthrough innovation that transforms user and consumer experiences, opens new business opportunities and new business models, and leverages data in the entirely new ways. Key initiatives such as Zero Distance, which focuses on finding innovation in every project for every client, on an ongoing basis, has set a precedent in the industry for driving grass root innovations. Similarly, the notion of looking at technology as an amplifier of human potential has enabled the company to bring together services, software, and platform in a way that drives unprecedented value for companies across every industry.

In addition, Mr Sikka has created a strong focus on learning and education within Infosys, a culture which not only drives value for clients and the entire Infosys ecosystem but extends outside the company as well. Infosys is helping clients in their efforts to create learning and collaborative cultures, helping them to find the most important problems to solve using design thinking as the framework, to rethink existing processes leveraging technology, to find new ways of working as teams and as individuals, and to build incredible talent, skills, and passion across teams.

Prior to joining Infosys, Mr Sikka was a member of the Executive Board of SAP SE, lead-in all products and technologies, including all of the product development, and driving innovation globally. In his 12 years at SAP, Mr Sikka held several senior leadership roles including becoming SAP's first-ever CTO in 2007. As CTO, Mr Sikka was responsible for overall technical architecture and ensuring coherence in SAP's five product strategies. During that time and later when he joined the Executive Board of SAP, Mr Sikka brought a strong focus on delivering innovative non-disruptively (delivering non -disruptive innovation), simplifying customers landscapes, and delivering new and delightful user experiences.

When Mr Sikka joined the SAP Executive Board in February 2010, he brought this same focus to all of the product development and was instrumental in building a culture of innovation at SAP; innovation became the focus and was at the heart of everything the company developed and delivered to customers. Among other things, Mr Sikka is credited with creating SAP's breakthrough in-memory data platform SAP HANA, the fastest growing product in SAP's history. He also accelerated SAP's development processes, bringing a deep focus on design and user experience, creating a culture of innovation, initiating for the first time in company history a focus on start-ups, driving venture investments, and leading product incubation as well as co-innovation with customers.

Mr Sikka is the creator of 'timeless software', a framework which articulates the principles of renewing existing processes and landscapes without disruption to customer environments. The principles of Timeless Software provide the foundation for ensuring there is a trade-off between leveraging breakthrough innovation and ensuring the consistency, reliability, and coherence of systems and user experiences. Mr Sikka is especially known for his championship of technology as an amplifier of human potential and his passion for applying the software in purposeful ways to address some of the biggest global challenges.

His experience includes research in artificial intelligence, intelligent systems, programming languages and models, and information management at Stanford University, at Xerox Palo Alto Labs, and as the founder of two start-ups.

Conflict between Narayana Murthy and Vishal Sikka

Publicly, and ostensibly, the Infosys fight has focused on issues of corporate governance. The issues that came to the fore included the 24-month severance package of former CFO Rajiv Bansal which Sikka is alleged to have initially tried to hush-up and the allegedly overvalued acquisition of Skava and Panaya for $120 million and $200 million. Apart from these, Murthy has voiced concern about Sikka's performance and his salary package, which he thought was too high.

Murthy even went on to criticize Sikka openly. 'All that I hear from at least three independent directors, including Mr. Ravi Venkatesan (co-chairman), are complaints about Mr. Sikka. They have told me umpteen times that Mr. Sikka is not a CEO material, but CTO material,' he said. To put Sikka's salary in perspective, here is the data of his peers. In 2015–2016, Sikka's take-home of Rs 48.73 crore (including bonus and incentives) is the highest among peers. In comparison, Mr N Chandrasekaran, TCS then MD and CEO, drew Rs 25.6 crore, including perks and variable pay, according to the data. Wipro's CEO Mr Abidali Neemuchwala's annual pay was a mere Rs 12 crore.

However, one has to remember that Sikka's pay packet does not violate any law. Neither has it been kept a secret from anyone. It was approved by Infosys' board of directors and has been disclosed in the company's annual report. It is also true that Sikka took home a salary which was 935 times the median pays at Infosys last fiscal. Murthy is miffed because his long-stated philosophy of 'compassionate capitalism' suggests the ratio should ideally be 50–60 times the median. Frankly, this is arbitrary and debatable. But one has to understand where Murthy is coming from too. In a house in Palo Alto, Sikka lives in style. For Narayana Murthy whose entire life is a story about frugality, such expenses are pure anathema. Murthy has been known to lead a simple life.

In any case, Sikka has left. And Nandan Nilekani is in the saddle. But as things stand today, the Infosys brand has taken a hit and clients and investors are looking for more clarity.

In the final analysis, Sikka should have a copy of Sudha Murthy's novel Dollar Bahu. If Sikka had read the novel, he would have got a better understanding of the value system of the Murthys. Their sense of right and wrong. Their Spartan worldview and their humble philosophy—simple living and high thinking.

Mr Narayana Murthy Values—simple living and high thinking.

N.R. Narayana Murthy is the legendary co-founder and retired chairman of Indian tech giant Infosys, in which he continues to hold a minority stake. Murthy stepped down as chairman in 2011 after 30 years with the company but returned in 2013 to hand over management to a professional CEO in 2014. In 2017, Murthy was in the news for raising concerns over alleged corporate governance lapses at Infosys, which the company denied. The controversy led to the CEO's resignation and a board shake-up, which saw the return of retired co-founder Nandan Nilekani as non-executive chairman.

Back to Mr Salil Parekh in His Office

Infosys Ltd, India's second-largest IT services exporter, has its sixth CEO in its 36-year history. Mr Salil Parekh is the second non-founder CEO hired at the company after an acrimonious stint by his predecessor Mr Vishal Sikka. Parekh inherits a company with several serious strengths including high margins, a large customer, and employee base. He also has several immediate challenges.

Customer Outreach: While services contracts are typically spread over several years and there is no immediate danger, customers are usually wary when vendor firms undergo turbulence. Parekh's first priority is to talk to key customers and reassure them that everything is hunky-dory and he is in control of the situation.

Working relationship with founders: Vishal Sikka was felled by his lack of a good relationship with the founders. The founders might hold only a small percentage (about 12%) of the company but cast a long shadow on the company's functioning. So Parekh needs to work out clearly red lines and open clear lines of communication with the founders and the Board.

Improve employee morale: All the recent tumult has left employees with low morale. He needs to reassure them that they and the company have a bright future.

Strategy: Parekh will also need to review strategy and come to a conclusion whether he wants to chart a different course from what Sikka laid out or move faster on the same path. Either way he needs to seriously look at strategy and market tactics.

Restore stakeholder trust: Infosys for long was seen as a torchbearer for corporate governance, a reputation which took a strong beating in the recent fracas. He will have to talk to other stakeholders including investors, analysts, and market watchers on restoring company's reputation.

Case Questions

1. Do you think that Mr Sikka was a misfit in the company? How will you rate him as CEO?

2. What are the main lessons for Mr. Parekh like the need to understanding and adopting the Corporate culturecat Infosys?

3. How the company should do damage control for its tarnished reputation?

18

Microsoft's Acquisition of Nokia

Learning Objectives

To understand the concept of merger and acquisition and its implications on strategy, technology, marketing, and financial intents, IP acquisition, and licenses. To understand the role of PESTEL factors and SWOT analysis in strategic decision making.

Synopsis

In September 2013, US-based computing major, Microsoft Corp. (Microsoft) and Finland-based communications company, Nokia Corporation (Nokia), announced that both the companies would enter into a transaction where Microsoft would acquire Nokia's devices and services segment, license Nokia's patents and license and use Nokia's mapping services, for US$ 7.2 billion.

Earlier in February 2011, Nokia had entered into a strategic alliance with Microsoft in a bid to combine the traditional strengths of the two companies to create synergies. With the acquisition of Nokia, Microsoft aimed to build on its partnership with the former by accelerating the growth of its share and profit in mobile devices through faster innovation, increased synergies, and unified branding and marketing.

The case analyses and highlights the acquisition strategy from the strategic fit perspective as well as the benefits/advantages envisaged by both the companies.

Indian Business Case Studies. V P Pawar, Bhagyashree Kunte, and Srinivas Tumuluri, Oxford University Press.
© ASM Group of Institutes, Pune, India 2022. DOI: 10.1093/oso/9780192869388.003.0018

Strategic Imperatives for M&A

M&A continues to be one of the most favoured routes adopted by corporations to further expand their market, the number of shareholders, and other strategic interests. In a merger one of the two existing companies merges its identity into another existing company or one or more existing companies may form a new company and merge their identities into a new company by transferring their businesses and undertakings including all other assets and liabilities to the new company (hereinafter referred to as the merged company). Whereas, acquisitions are often made as part of a company's growth strategy whereby it is more beneficial to take over an existing firm's operations and niche status compared to expanding on its own. In scenarios where expansion into new markets come with significant risks encompassing time and effort in gaining a foothold, M&A prove to be an instant success mantra to catapult into a dominating force within the market. Curiously though, chances of success remain extremely low. Plausible reasons attributed to failures in M&A range from over-optimism to outright over-spending displayed by the management leading to an exacerbated purchase consideration to the target firm with limited regard to realization of synergy. Notwithstanding the historical evidence suggesting overwhelmingly large number of failures, corporations that have engaged in M&A while being thoroughly mindful of the aspirations of the shareholders of the acquiring firm have tasted enormous success. Such corporations have avidly resisted the temptation to overpay and also built strategies to lead harmonious integration across people, processes, and resources subsequent to acquisition of target entities.

Microsoft's Story towards Acquisition of Nokia

Microsoft has traditionally been associated with production of highly efficient software product with the everywhere. 'Windows' that has virtually become a household name in respect of computing technology. However, the rapid strides made by 'open software' and competitors like Apple giving the conventional market leader a run for its money explains the urgency on part of Microsoft in proceeding ahead with the acquisition. With smartphone almost becoming an equivalent of a hand-held 'computer', companies like Apple have found themselves in a brilliant spot where they are dispensed with the ability to embed their proprietary software into the smartphone. With Apple itself manufacturing the smartphone, it becomes a natural extension of their backward integration strategy. While the transition to a product-led growth seemed natural for Microsoft, it must be noted that Apple always had a superior competitive advantage with Apple already having tasted stupendous success on the front of i-pods and i-pads. Microsoft, on the other hand, was relatively a new entrant in the technology-led product space from a strictly conventional sense. The fact that Nokia was too late in adapting to the latest innovations engineered by its competitor only meant that the company was staring at the undesirable prospect of a complete rout of the market leadership that it once championed.

In April 2010 Nokia introduced its next flagship mobile device, the Nokia N8, which would be the first to run on Symbian. However it was delayed for many months which marked the company's image. On 10 September 2010, Olli-Pekka Kallasvuo was fired as CEO and it was announced that Stephen Elop from Microsoft would take Nokia's CEO position, becoming the first non-Finnish director in Nokia's history. Nokia's Symbian platform that had been the leading smartphone platform in Europe and Asia for many years was quickly becoming outdated and difficult for developers after the advent of iOS and Android. To counter this, Nokia planned to make their MeeGo Linux operating system the company's flagship on smartphones. However, in February 2011, they scrapped MeeGo and announced a partnership with Microsoft to use Windows Phone as Nokia's primary operating system, relegating Symbian to a lower priority. Although the MeeGo-based N9 was met with a highly positive reception in 2011, Nokia—apparently pressured by Microsoft—had already decided to end development on MeeGo and solely focus on its Microsoft partnership. After the announcement of the Microsoft deal, Nokia's market share deteriorated; this was due to demand for Symbian dropping when consumers realized Nokia's focus and attention would be elsewhere. Nokia's first Windows Phone flagship was the Lumia 800, which arrived in November 2011.

Falling sales in 2011, which were not being improved significantly with the Lumia line in 2012, led to consecutive quarters of huge losses. By mid-2012, with the company's stock price falling below $2, Nokia almost became bankrupt.

On 11 March 2011 Nokia announced that it had paid Elop a $6 million signing bonus as 'compensation for lost income from his prior employer', on top of his $1.4 million annual salary. This was a turning point, since Elop has previously been a Microsoft employee in its Business Division. It later became clear that Microsoft was influential within Nokia, pushing forward its Windows Phone offering. When the Lumia 920 was announced in September 2012, it was seen by the press as the first high-end Windows Phone that could challenge rivals due to its advanced feature set. The company was also making gains in developing countries with its Asha series, which were selling strongly. Although Nokia's smartphone market share recovered in 2013, it was still not enough to improve the dire financial situation the company had had huge losses for two years, and in September 2013 announced the sale of its mobile and devices division to Microsoft. The sale was positive for Nokia to stop further disastrous financial figures, as well as for Microsoft's CEO Steve Ballmer, who wanted Microsoft to produce more hardware and turn it into a devices and services company. The sale was completed in April 2014, with Microsoft Mobile becoming the successor to Nokia's mobile devices division.

Failure of Microsoft and Nokia M&A

After the sale of its mobile devices division, Nokia focused on network equipment through Nokia Networks. In October 2014, Nokia and China Mobile signed a US$970 million framework deal for delivery between 2014 and 2015. On 17 November 2014, Nokia Technologies head Ramzi Haidamus disclosed that the company planned to re-enter the consumer electronics business as an original design manufacturer, licensing in-house hardware designs, and technologies to third-party manufacturers. The next day, Nokia unveiled the N1, an Android tablet manufactured by Foxconn, as its first product following the Microsoft sale. Haidamus emphasized that devices released under these licensing agreements would be held to high standards in production quality, and would 'look and feel just like Nokia built it'. Nokia CEO Rajeev Suri stated that the company planned to re-enter the mobile phone business in this manner in 2016, following the expiration of its non-compete clause with Microsoft.

The company took aggressive steps to revitalize itself, evident through its hiring of software experts, testing of new products, and seeking of sales partners. On 14 July 2015, CEO Rajeev Suri confirmed that the company would make a return to the mobile phones market in 2016.

On 18 May 2016, Microsoft Mobile sold its Nokia-branded feature phone business to HMD Global, a new company founded by former Nokia executive Jean-Francois Baril, and an associated factory in Vietnam to Foxconn's FIH Mobile subsidiary. Nokia subsequently entered into a long-term licensing deal to make HMD the exclusive manufacturer of Nokia-branded phones and tablets outside Japan, operating in conjunction with Foxconn. The deal also granted HMD the right to essential patents and feature phone software.

Future Prospects of Nokia

HMD subsequently announced the Android-based Nokia 6 smartphone in January 2017. At Mobile World Congress, HMD additionally unveiled the Nokia 3 and Nokia 5 smartphones, as well as a re-imagining of Nokia's classic 3310 feature phone. While Nokia has no investment in the company they do have some input in the new devices.

On 28 June 2016 Nokia demonstrated for the first time ever a 5G-ready network. In February 2017 Nokia carried out a 5G connection in Oulu, Finland using the 5GTF standard, backed by Verizon, on Intel architecture-based equipment.

On 5 July 2017, Nokia and Xiaomi announced that they have signed a business collaboration agreement and a multi-year patent agreement, including a cross-license to each company's cellular standard essential patents.

On 19 January 2018, Nokia signed a deal with NTT Docomo, Japan's largest mobile operator, to provide 5G wireless radio base stations in the country by 2020.

Case Questions

1. Will Microsoft develop products with high and reliable quality after the acquisition sufficient to rise in the smartphone market?

2. Will Microsoft's deal with Nokia produce a significant impact on the smartphone business?

3. What are the reasons for failure of merger and acquisition between Microsoft and Nokia?

4. Do you think Nokia made mistake selling stake to Microsoft?

5. Do research on current mobile markets scenario—major players and SWOT analysis.

19

The Pains of Separation

A Case Study Highlighting the Plight of Several Executives Rendered Jobless (Downsizing)

Learning Objectives

Today businesses and organizations face relentless pressures to become leaner. Such demands are the result of global competition and rapid technology change. Many organizations have responded by corporate restructuring and downsizing, often 'spinning off' divisions originally part of the larger scheme of things. The logic is, when you demerge different units, each unit can focus on specific areas of business, sharply improving their prospects in the larger marketplace. And if the stock prices of the recently demerged entities in the country are anything to go by, the market has definitely given a thumbs-up to most demergers.

Synopsis

One of the more visible signs of organizational restructuring is that many firms have become flatter on the organizational chart. In search of efficiencies, some of them have removed entire layers of management to speed up communication and reduce headcount. So far so good. But what often ends up roiling the water is the prospect of employee redundancy (HP, which is headed for a split, may cut around 55,000 jobs globally), redeployments, and job separation as a company gets into the restructuring mode. A review of literature on spin-offs and demergers seems to suggest that a split in business can be organizationally disruptive as it can cause stress and broken bonds between employees who feel vulnerable

Indian Business Case Studies. V P Pawar, Bhagyashree Kunte, and Srinivas Tumuluri, Oxford University Press.
© ASM Group of Institutes, Pune, India 2022. DOI: 10.1093/oso/9780192869388.003.0019

and not in control of their careers. Given this, experts suggest corporate leaders must ask some fundamental questions before embarking on a de-merger exercise: How can the company work to minimize the human impact of a demerger while remaining competitive? Indeed, how does the psychological contract between the worker and the employer change post a split? Above all, how can the workforce be motivated to perform better after the split?

It must be understood that regardless of whether an organization conceptualizes and designates its spin-off as re-engineering or re-organization of business, the adoption and implementation of workforce reorientation strategies will inexorably produce considerable financial, organizational, and emotional effects. While some such outcomes can be anticipated and are tangible, others have unexpected, long-term consequences that are difficult to measure.

Back to Basics

The corporate restructuring exercises (including demergers) have deep psychological scars on employees (existing and the outgoing ones). Cascio, who is a professor of Management at the University of Colorado, says that to mitigate the risks companies must begin by asking a simple question: Are we facing a short-term crisis or do we think that our business needs to undergo fundamental structural changes in that we need new plans and new strategy, a complete overhauling to move forward? In other words, to make the move successful, the organization needs to set out the goals clearly before embarking on a demerger—or any other manner of restructuring—exercise.

Once the business leader is clear in his mind on what the objective is, the expectation from the employees becomes easier to set. According to Sridhar Ganesan, country head, Hay Group India, while the demerger mandate is always clear most of the time—to grow the business in a completely independent landscape—it is the mind shift of employees that needs to be plotted carefully before the restructuring takes place. 'Employees can be concerned about their roles in view of the talent movement that will take place. The accountability of the new company also goes up with the pressure to perform better,' he adds.

The best way to deal with this scenario is through communication. Crystal clear communication, to be precise. This means the HR has to be taken into confidence early on in the process so that it can chalk out a communication roadmap for the people who stay back, for the people who move on, and for those who must go.

See how Future Group managed its demerger exercise. In 2012, Pantaloon Retail India and Future Ventures India decided to demerge their lifestyle fashion businesses into Future Fashion. Given the speed at which the company was restructuring (it further demerged its businesses in fashion, hypermarket, and food) even altering its business model time and again, it was natural for the employees to feel uneasy. Looking at the growing restlessness and uncertainty among employees, the company management took two key decisions pretty early on its course—first, that it had to 'talk' to the people; and second, that all communication had to flow from one common source that would filter down to the last employee, even those operating from the shop floor.

To this end, the company announced a special-purpose telephone number, dialling which any employee could get in touch with Future Group's founder Kishore Biyani. Additionally, every Friday Biyani addressed and updated the employees on the company's plans. Videos were shot specifically targeting the shop floor staff, in which Biyani briefed his employees about the latest developments at the company. The whole exercise was orchestrated in a manner that people felt they knew what was going on leaving little room for speculation. 'We constantly sought feedback from people, tried to understand how we could add value to the employee's role in the restructuring phase,' says Kaustubh Sonalkar, head, people office.

Future Group planned meticulously over five quarters, the demerger process left very few casualties in its wake. The best part, according to the company, was that there were no lay-offs, zero attrition. 'The HR team had so much data that it could distribute roles and job opportunities within the organisation,' says Sonalkar who agrees that many Indian companies still need to refine the systems and processes to make a demerger smooth. 'The spotlight cannot be only on the shareholders; you have to understand that value erosion can happen when employees are dissatisfied or asked to leave,' he adds.

According to independent HR consultant Gautam Ghosh, 'A corporate spin-off is not necessarily bad news for employees. The problem is that many organizations do not communicate a demerger strategy to their employees proactively. In fact, in my experience, even some MNCs, known otherwise for their professional management practices, fail to share a clear roadmap with their country or regional offices making the whole process painful and fraught with risks.'

Ghosh warns communication that is one-way is not good enough. 'A company that runs a global business should consult the leaders of all the countries to assess the HR implications of tough business decisions. This will help them avoid bad press,' adds Ghosh.

Analysts say that companies that have split businesses successfully in recent years—such as Marico, Crompton Greaves, Polaris, and Wipro—have planned well and have been rewarded handsomely. Some of them have even helped outgoing employees via out-placements with the promise that they can return at an appropriate time in the future.

That said, the communication strategy has to be more refined. Gurupreet Singh, country head, YSC India, an HR facilitator, points out that some organizations tend to procrastinate on breaking the news relating to far-reaching changes in the organization by design. 'Demergers can create confusion among employees and affect the company's performance at the stock market. Responsible companies must know that it is the employees who have to finally bear the impact of such decisions, some of them may have to pay a heavy price if things go off-track. So it is best if the people know the facts before the shareholders do.'

Rajiv Kapoor, chief people officer at Fortis Healthcare, adds, 'Not informing employees timely about demergers could be a ploy to get rid of some part of the workforce. This includes employees who will start looking for opportunities outside the organization at the sign of trouble. This will ease the downsizing drive.'

Clearly then, the success of a business split boils down to transparency and clear conversation between the employer and the employees. The secret sauce is to tick all the boxes relevant for any restructuring exercise: preparing early, putting together a transition team, focusing on clear communication, and knowing that engagement (even with outgoing employees) won't be over even after you have gone through the legal routine.

Look before You Split

Separation can be painful. When planned carefully, the rewards are huge. Here are six things to think about:

- Use the demerger exercise as an opportunity to address long-term problems. You need to clearly understand why the demerger is taking place after all. Invest time in assessing the impact on those who are moved to the new entity, and the ability of the organization to serve its customers. Answer questions like what systems will be in place for the demerged company? What will be the support from the parent company in the initial phase of operations? What tools will the HR use to communicate with the employees so that the best talent is retained and no one feels short-changed?
- Before taking a final call on the split, ask employees about their concerns and seek their input. Never underestimate the value of asking your employees for ideas. Even if their ideas do not make good business sense and cannot be put into action, you, as the employer, will have demonstrated to your workers that they matter. Make special efforts to solicit the input of 'star' employees or opinion leaders within the organization, for they can help communicate the rationale for the impending restructuring to their fellow employees and promote trust in the restructuring effort. Involve the HR team right at the outset, ask for their inputs in developing the communication that would eventually filter down to employees.
- Keep the channels of communication open while retaining focus on both the employee and the customer. Make employees understand why a new entity is being carved out, or why a division needs to have its own identity instead of being seen as a 'liability'. Explain to customers why a separation from the parent company is important. Communicate in a variety of ways in order to keep everyone abreast of new developments. Executives should be visible, active

participants in this process, and be sure that lower-level managers are trained to address the concerns of victims as well as survivors.

- If layoffs are necessary, make decisions in a consistent manner to ensure that employees perceive the process as fair. Before laying off employees, be sure that you have looked at all the options, including asking your employees whether they would be willing to make 'small sacrifices' for the good of the company. Employees can show surprising loyalty and flexibility if they perceive their employer to be fair. Try to retain your best performers, and provide maximum advance notice to employees whose services you need to terminate. Ensure that management at all levels shares the pain and participates in any sacrifices employees are asked to bear.

- Keep the communication going even after the demerger is complete. It could be an idea for HR teams, among other teams, to continue communicating with the people till both the companies achieve stability. This will minimize disturbances to both the parent and the demerged company and reduce speculation.

- Examine all systems and processes in the light of the change of strategy or environment facing the firm. Train employees and their managers in the new ways of operating. There is enough evidence to show that firms in which training budgets are increased following a restructuring are more likely to see improved productivity.

Conclusions

The efforts of larger groups of companies to exit from non-core businesses and spinoff smaller noncore group companies to meet renewed investment demands for core business activity especially due to disruptive changes due to technological changes in terms of globally competitive AI-driven product and process lines are creating havoc in the career plans of many executives due to uncertainty of their employment as also redundancy of their skill sets. The senior you are more is the risk since you are less amenable to learn and adapt to new skill sets. It therefore necessary for the management and the employees to be cautious, aware, and proactive of consequences of demergers and spinoff strategies.

Case Questions

1. What should be the strategy for employees rehabilitation incase few of them get to be displaced due to organizations demerger or spinoff strategies?

2. What are the proactive strategies to avoid separation due to change in product, process, and marketing technology. How do you take care of loyal senior-level employees?

3. Disruptive changes are there to stay in every market segment. How should the employees work out their career plans since they are likely to be affected by disruptive changes?

20

What Went Wrong?

A Case Study on Nestle Maggi Noodles

Learning Objectives

The present case helps to study the issues involved in sustaining the image of a popular brand and how to rebuild a brand in a crisis situation. It also helps to learn the need and importance of brand extension. The case also helps to understand the effect of negative marketing on the brands' image. The major objective of this case study is to learn the various strategies adopted for brand repositioning of Maggi noodles by Nestle.

Synopsis

Maggi the trusted and valuable food brand in India is the favourite among all the children in the country. It was considered as snacks in many households and a basic diet in many other homes. But in the recent past, the ban on Maggi has created a negative impact of Nestle. The favourite and most preferred instant food product of children, Maggi Noodles, got entangled in its ethical issues of the ingredients being used. The corporate social responsibility of Nestle India was tremendously cross-questioned with its after test results, by food regulatory authorities. The case study is an effort to explore the various issues, possibilities, and opportunities for Maggi. The study focuses on need and scope brand image and brand repositioning, brand extension, etc.

Indian Business Case Studies. V P Pawar, Bhagyashree Kunte, and Srinivas Tumuluri, Oxford University Press.
© ASM Group of Institutes, Pune, India 2022. DOI: 10.1093/oso/9780192869388.003.0020

Implementation Details

The company used various social media channels to take care of its image while the media was putting questions on its image.

- Initially company rejected the accusation that the noodles were unsafe and said on their website and social media accounts that there had been no order to recall any products. A statement on their website said 'The quality and safety of our products are the top priorities for our Company. We have in place strict food safety and quality controls at out Maggi factories. We do not add MSG to Maggi Noodles, and glutamate, if present, may come from naturally occurring sources. We are surprised with the content supposedly found in the sample as we monitor the lead content regularly as a part of the regulatory requirements.'
- Nestle continued to keep its customers up to date on the investigation into the safety of Maggi noodles in India. Nestle stated on the official Maggi noodles Facebook page, Twitter, and website, that extensive testing revealed no excess lead in Maggi noodles.
- Nestle used its Twitter and Facebook accounts to answer customers' questions about the levels of MSG and lead found in their noodles. The company continued to reassure customers that the noodles are safe and that they are a transparent company working closely with authorities in India to resolve the issue.
- Nestle recalled all Maggi noodles from India. After re-assuring customers that its noodles are safe, the brand did a U-turn and decided to recall Maggi noodles from the shelves. CEO Paul Bulcke said, 'We are working with authorities to clarify the situation and in the meantime Nestle will be withdrawing Maggi noodles from shelves.'
- Nestle decided to destroy more than $50 million worth of Maggi noodles in India after they were deemed unsafe by regulators.

Even as people back in India are left craving for their favourite instant noodles Maggi, reports said that the India Research Center of Harvard Business School (HBS) will conduct a case study on the noodles.

The case study, will discuss what led to the recall of the noodles, may be completed within a month, which is quite quick compared to the nine months that HBS takes to complete such studies.

Maggi, something that Indians had come to love since it was launched in the early 90s, was taken off the shelves after it was found to have high lead content.

HBS has approached several stakeholders. The report quoted an official as saying, 'We have been approached for comment on the Nestle Maggi mess.' The official spoke on the condition of anonymity.

And while Maggi has been off the shelves for over two months now, a Bombay High Court order had quashed the ban on Maggi noodles and ordered fresh tests.

However, the government had said the verdict did not alter the grounds on which it had claimed Rs 640 crore in damages from Nestle for misleading advertisement and unfair trade practices.

The Food Safety and Standards Authority of India (FSSAI) too were still convinced about why the ban was imposed on the instant noodles brand. The regulator maintained that the ban was imposed after thorough tests on the products, and had questioned Nestle's extensive disposal of existing Maggi stock.

On behalf of the consumers, the Food and Consumer Affairs Ministry separately filed a Class Action Suit against Nestle India before the National Consumer Disputes Redressed Commission (NCDRC), using a hitherto unused provision in the three-decade-old Consumer Protection Act. In the case the centre had claimed damages worth Rs 640 crore.

The ministry had sought Rs 284.45 crore in basic damages and further Rs 355.50 crore in punitive damages, resulting in total damages of Rs 639.95 crore from the Swiss giant.

Nestle, which had to recall the popular noodles brand after orders from the central food safety regulator FSSAI and food regulators in various states, is the first foreign firm in India to face a class action suit.

With the launch of Maggi noodles, NIL created an entirely new food category—instant noodles—in the Indian packaged food market. Because of its first-mover advantage, NIL successfully managed to retain its leadership in the instant noodles category even until the early 2000s.

Over the years, NIL extended the Maggi brand to a variety of culinary products like soups, sauces and ketchups, and cooking aids among others. However, these product extensions were not as successful as the instant noodles. In 2005, NIL started offering a range of new 'healthy' products under the Maggi brand, in a bid to attract health-conscious consumers.

This case looks at the various phases in the product life cycle of Maggi noodles in India. It talks about the various measures taken by NIL to keep the Maggi brand fresh in the minds of Indian consumers. The case also talks about the various extensions of the Maggi brand and tries to analyse why only the sauces and ketchups category, among all the other product extensions, managed to succeed. It further discusses the measures taken by NIL to reposition Maggi as a 'health product'. The case ends with a discussion of whether NIL would be successful in sustaining this new image for Maggi in the market.

When Maggi was deemed unsafe in India, all eyes were on Nestle to see how they would respond and manage the situation. Nestle defended its product on all social media channels and rejected all claims that its noodles were unsafe. They used the best use of social media to connect the masses. Initially the websites which were used for promotion of the product was now being used for maintaining its image.

- Maggi India's Twitter account makes an impressive effort to respond to every tweet from customers on this issue with a pre-prepared statement explaining that lead occurs naturally in soil and water. Nestle also explained the science behind the reason for the ban in simple terms so customers could understand.
- The scare was a huge blow to the company, which has been selling its Maggi products for over three decades in India with 80% of the country's instant noodle market. However, through smart use of social media during the crisis, the brand limited further damage by reassuring and informing customers to encourage them to continue buying the noodles in the future.
- Nestle India is preparing a blueprint for a possible re-launch of the Maggi instant noodles brand. Industry experts and analysts feel the issue of the recall and ban of Maggi noodles in India is likely to be resolved in the next three to six months.

Customer Expectations

Your customers expect you to deliver quality products. If you do not, they will quickly look for alternatives. Quality is critical to satisfying your customers and retaining their loyalty so they continue to buy from you in the future. Quality products make an important contribution to long-term revenue and profitability. They also enable you to charge and maintain higher prices.

Reputation

Quality influences your company's reputation. The growing importance of social media means that customers and prospects can easily share both favourable opinions and criticism of your product quality on forums, product review sites, and social networking sites, such as Facebook and Twitter. A strong reputation for quality can be an important differentiator in markets that are very competitive. Poor quality or a product failure that results in a product recall campaign can create negative publicity and damage your reputation.

Meeting Standards

Accreditation to a recognized quality standard may be essential for dealing with certain customers or complying with legislation. Public sector companies, for example, may insist that their suppliers achieve accreditation with quality standards. If you sell products in regulated markets, such as health care, food, or electrical goods, you must be able to comply with health and safety standards designed to protect consumers. Accredited quality control systems play a crucial role in complying with those standards. Accreditation can also help you win new customers or enter new markets by giving prospects independent confirmation of your company's ability to supply quality products.

Costs

Poor quality increases costs. If you do not have an effective quality control system in place, you may incur the cost of analysing non-conforming goods or services to determine the root causes and retesting products after reworking them. In some cases, you may have to scrap defective products and incur additional production costs to replace them. If defective products reach customers, you will have to pay for returns and replacements and, in serious cases; you could incur legal costs for failure to comply with customer or industry standards.

Why Is Branding Important?

So what is branding? And why is it so important for your business?

Branding goes way beyond just a logo or graphic element. When you think about your brand, you really want to think about your entire customer experience, everything from your logo, your website, your social media experiences, the way you answer the phone, to the way your customers experience your staff. When you look at this broad definition of branding, it can be a bit overwhelming to think about what is involved in your brand.

In short, your brand is the way your customer perceives you.

It is critical to be aware of your brand experience and have a plan to create the brand experience that you want to have a good brand doesn't just happen, it is a well thought out and strategic plan.

Many small organizations and start-ups neglect spending necessary time thinking about their brand in this broad sense and the impact it has on their business. Let's look at 10 reasons why digging into your brand is important:

Branding promotes recognition.

People tend to do business with companies they are familiar with. If your branding is consistent and easy to recognize, it can help people feel more at ease purchasing your products or services.

Your brand helps set you apart from the competition.

In today's global market, it is critical to stand apart from the crowd. You are no longer competing on a local stage; your organization now competes in the global economy. How do you stand out from the thousands or millions of similar organizations around the world?

Your brand tells people about your business DNA.

Your full brand experience, from the visual elements like the logo to the way that your phones are answered, tells your customer about the kind of company that you are. Are all of these points of entry telling the right story?

Your brand provides motivation and direction for your staff.

A clear brand strategy provides the clarity that your staff needs to be successful. It tells them how to act, how to win, and how to meet the organization's goals.

A strong brand generates referrals.

People love to tell others about the brands they like. People wear brands, eat brands, listen to brands, and they're constantly telling others about the brands they love. On the flip side, you can't tell someone about a brand you can't remember. 6. A strong brand is critical to generating referrals or viral traffic.

A strong brand helps customers know what to expect. A brand that is consistent and clear puts the customer at ease, because they know exactly what to expect each and every time they experience the brand.

Conclusions

Nestle has suffered from a big crisis because of food safety issues, which has damaged its brand image in the market. To overcome these crises they decided to go for brand extension and improving quality. Nestle should adopt more strategies to reposition their brand in the market like social media marketing, advertising, public relations, etc. They also have to do SWOT (Strength, Weakness, Opportunities, Threats) analysis at present situation to tackle with future competition.

Case Questions

1. Discuss the role of social media marketing in brand repositioning of Maggi noodles, in the context of present case.

2. What strategies Nestle should adopt to rebuild its brand image in the market?

3. What strategies should Nestle adopt to compete with the existing and new competitors?